PRODUCT SKETCHES

from rough to refined

andres parada

Expression through images has always felt most natural to me. When I was a young kid, I used pencils and crayons, as a teenager, it was often through a spray-can or acrylic paint, and since my mid-twenties, it has been through a pen or Photoshop.

I am not an educator, so this book is not intended to instruct. There are several books on the market right now that are doing a far better job than what I could do in instructing how to sketch, draw and render. My intent with this book is rather to inspire. For me, inspiration can be a great motivator. I remember as a child being inspired by older brother Pablo's drawings. He was so much better than me and he could draw things like Robin Hood, knights with mighty swords and the Hulk. That motivated me to want to draw more to improve my skills. I am by no means a master at sketching, drawing or visual communication, but I work diligently daily on honing my skills toward greater excellence. I firmly believe that the key to success in anything is hard work, diligence and consistency.

This book is divided into eight sections of content. Each section presents its topic from rough sketches done in an analog way to more refined sketches often created digitally in Photoshop. Most of the content in this book is non-client work, but all the sections are dedicated to areas of design in which I have some level of experience. My intent is to offer this compilation of sketch work as an inspirational and practical reference book that can motivate others to produce great work.

I hope you enjoy it,

Andres Parada 2013

SECTION 1

consumer
electronics

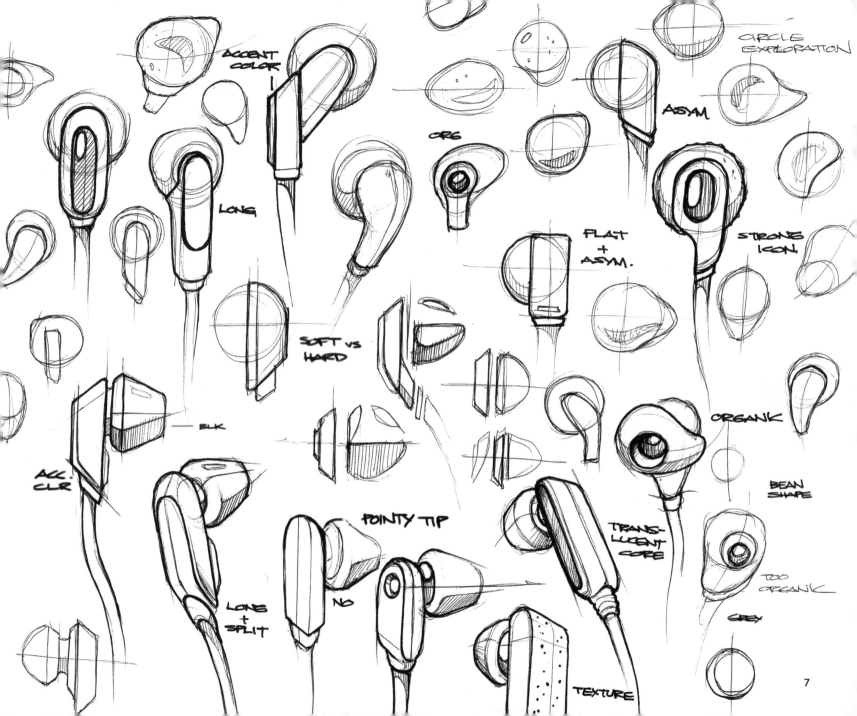

ACCENT COLOR

CIRCLE EXPLORATION

ASYM

LONG

ORG

FLAT + ASYM.

STRONG ICON.

SOFT vs HARD

ORGANIC

BLK

ACC. CLR

LONG + SPLIT

POINTY TIP

NO

BEAN SHAPE

TRANS-LUCENT CORE

TOO ORGANIC

GREY

TEXTURE

7

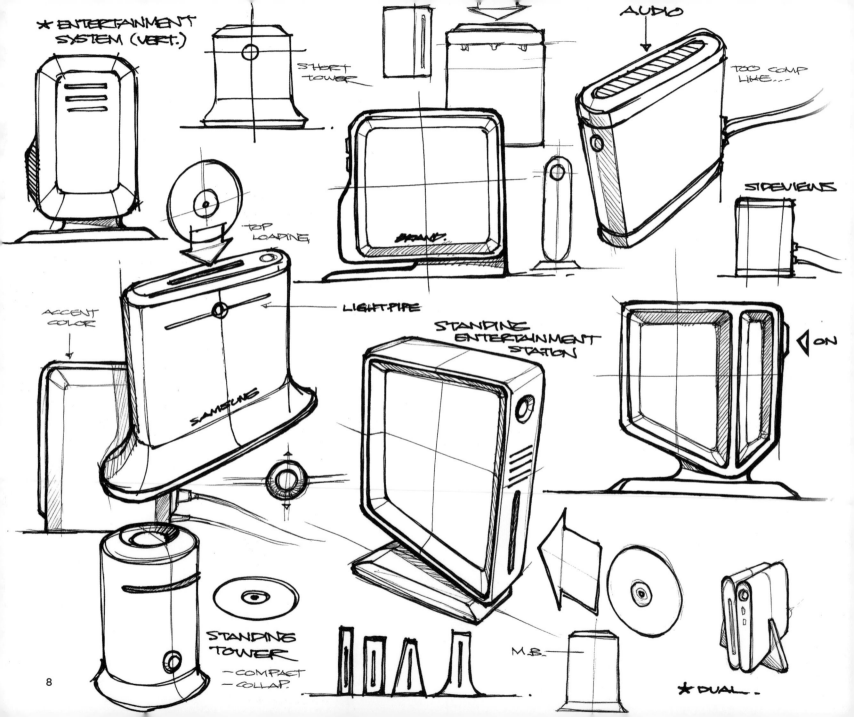

* ENTERTAINMENT SYSTEM (VERT.)

SHORT TOWER

AUDIO

TOO COMP LIKE...

SIDEVIEWS

TOP LOADING

LIGHT PIPE

ACCENT COLOR

SAMSUNG

STANDING ENTERTAINMENT STATION

ON

M.B.

STANDING TOWER
- COMPACT
- COLLAP.

* DUAL

8

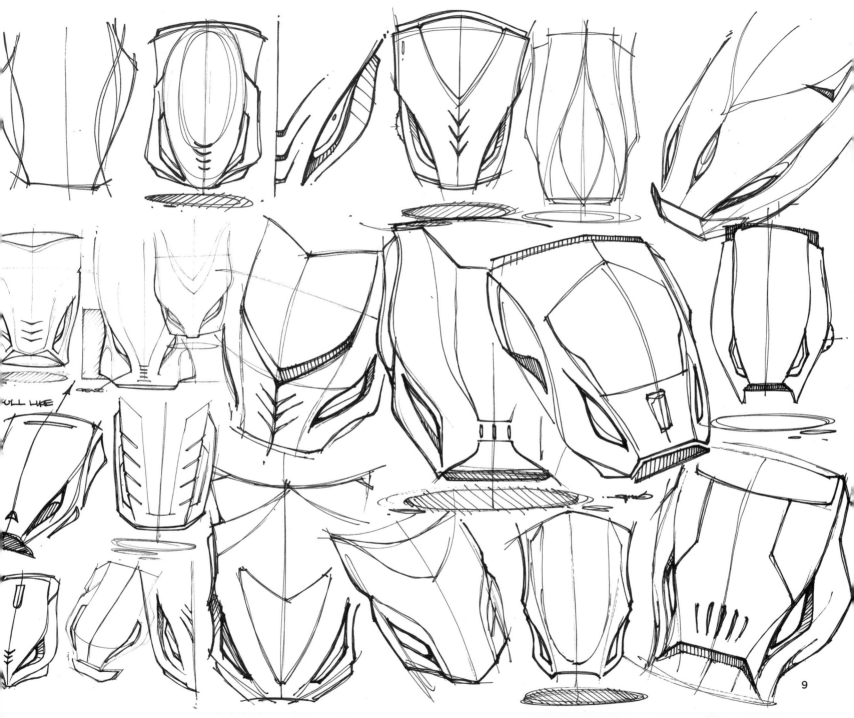

ULL LIKE

CREASE

9

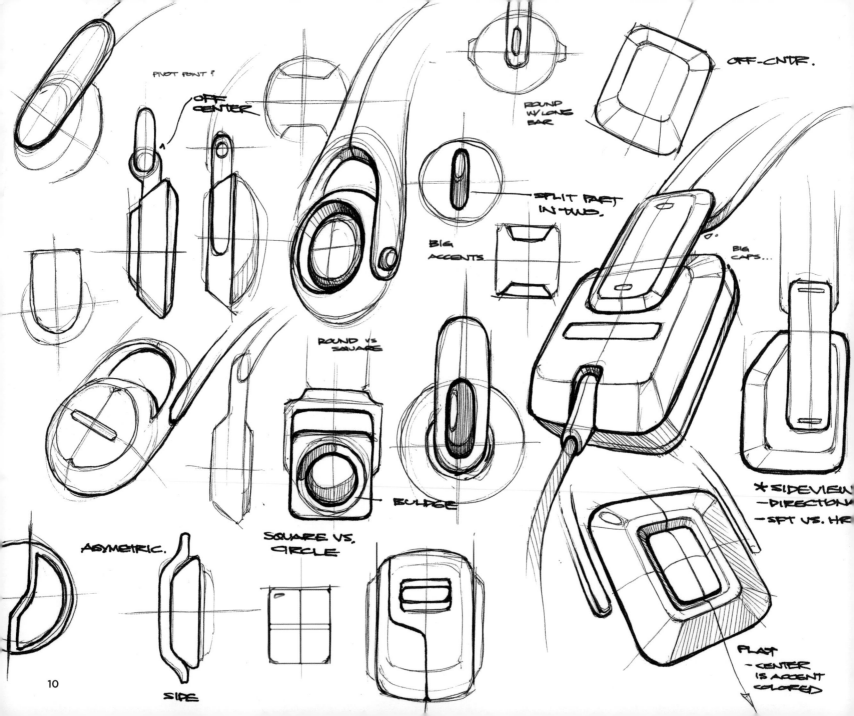

PIVOT POINT?

OFF CENTER

OFF-CNTR.

ROUND W/ LONG BAR

SPLIT PART IN-TWO.

BIG ACCENTS

BIG CAPS...

ROUND VS SQUARE

* SIDEVIEW
  - DIRECTION
  - SFT VS. HR

BULDGE

ASYMETRIC.

SQUARE VS. CIRCLE

FLAT
- CENTER IS ACCENT COLORED

SIDE

10

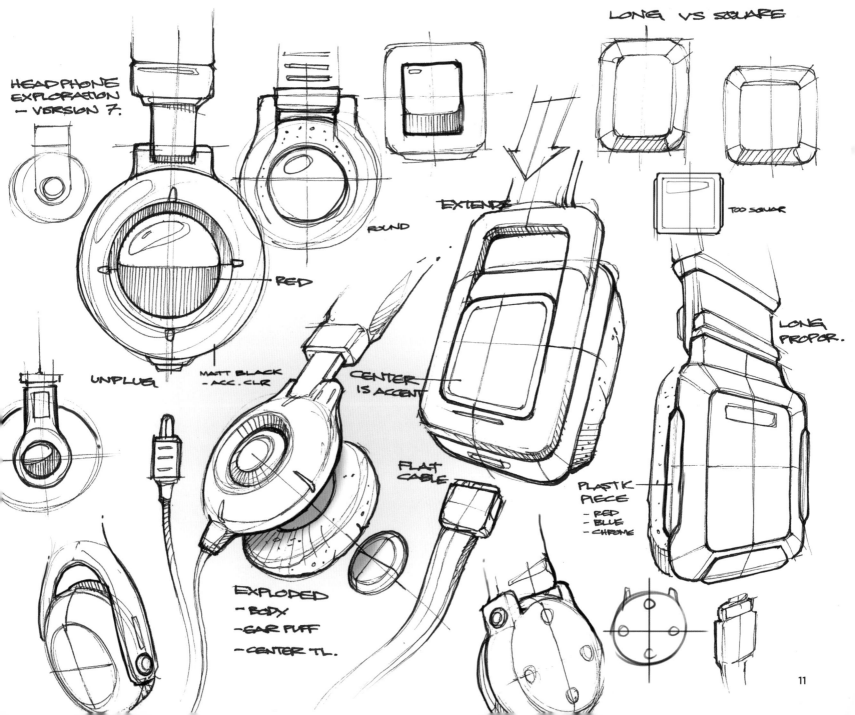

HEADPHONE
EXPLORATION
– VERSION 7.

RED

UNPLUG

MATT BLACK
– ACC. CLR

ROUND

EXTEND

CENTER
IS ACCENT

FLAT
CABLE

EXPLODED
– BODY
– EAR PUFF
– CENTER TL.

LONG VS SQUARE

TOO SQUAR

LONG
PROPOR.

PLASTIC
PIECE
– RED
– BLUE
– CHROME

11

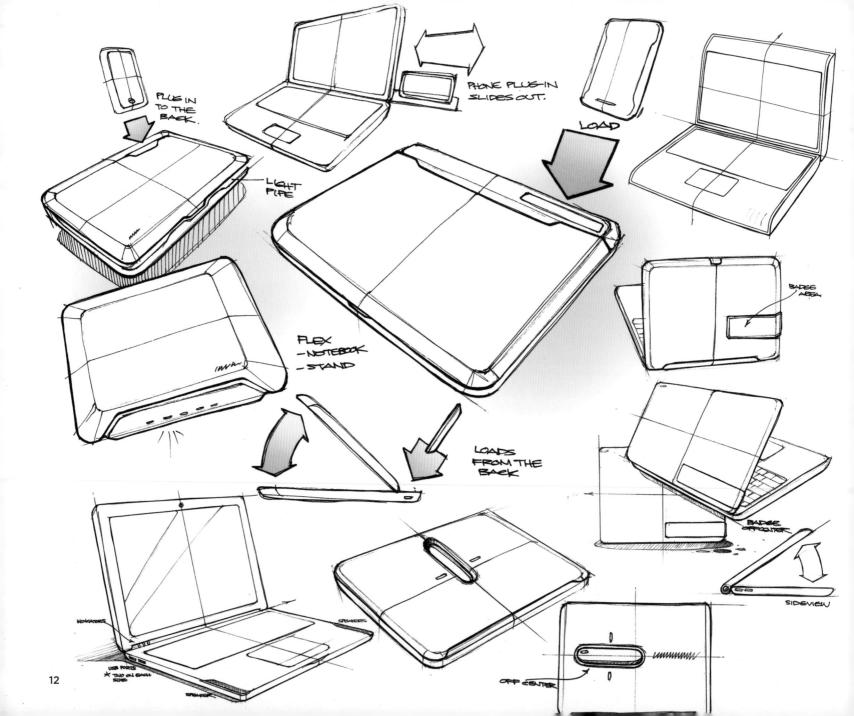

PLUG IN TO THE BACK.

PHONE PLUG-IN SLIDES OUT.

LOAD

LIGHT PIPE

BADGE AREA

FLEX
-NOTEBOOK
-STAND

LOADS FROM THE BACK

BADGE OFF CENTER

SIDEVIEW

INDICATORS

SPEAKERS

USB PORTS
★ TWO ON EACH SIDE

SPEAKER

OFF CENTER

12

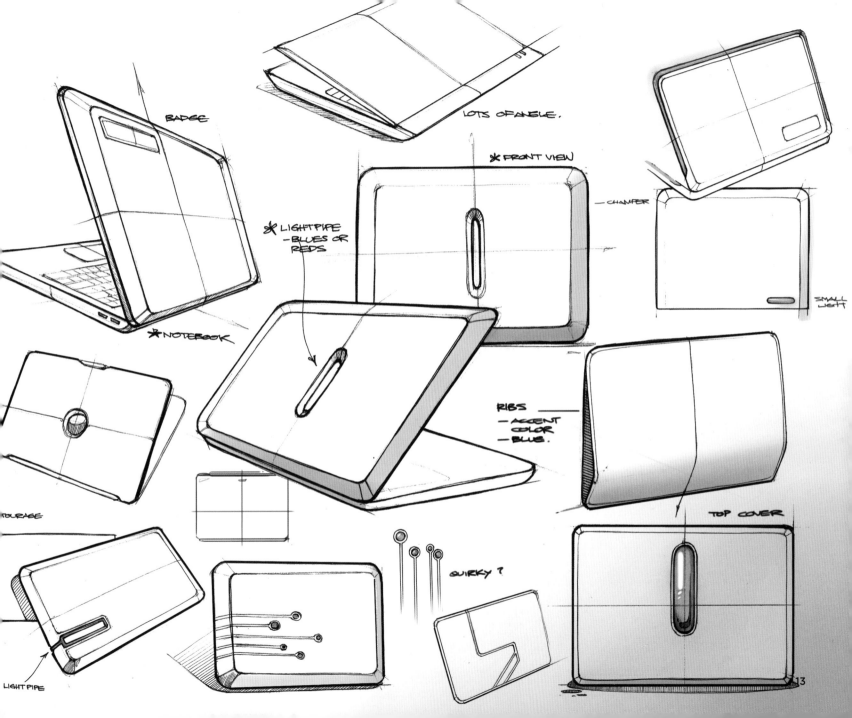

BADGE

LOTS OF ANGLE.

* FRONT VIEW

— CHAMFER

* LIGHTPIPE
- BLUES OR
REDS

SMALL
LIGHT

* NOTEBOOK

RIBS
- ACCENT
COLOR
- BLUE.

COURAGE

TOP COVER

LIGHT PIPE

QUIRKY ?

13

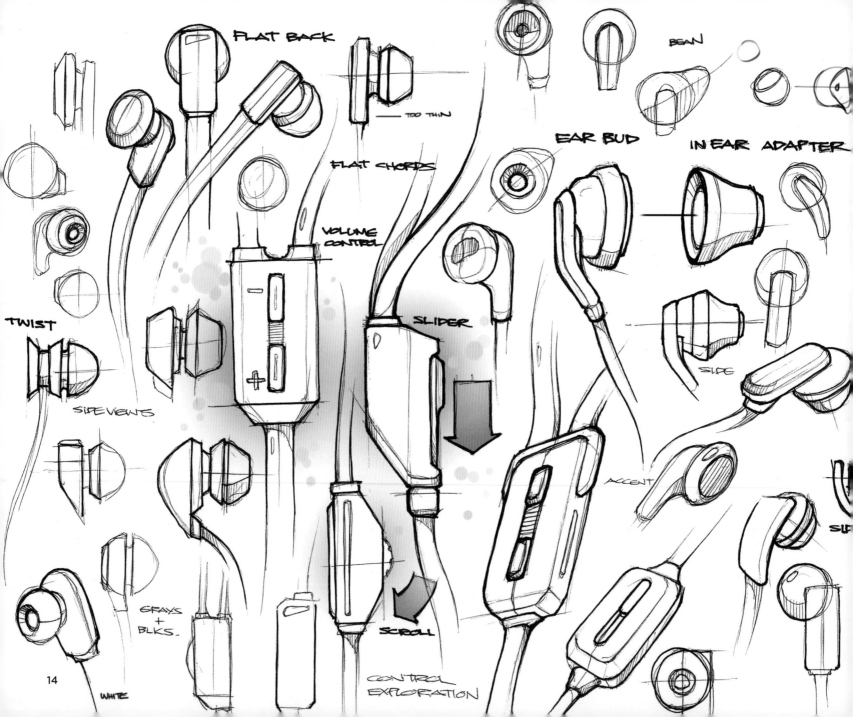

FLAT BACK

TOO THIN

BEAN

FLAT CHORDS

EAR BUD

IN EAR ADAPTER

VOLUME CONTROL

TWIST

SLIDER

SIDE VIEWS

ACCENT

SIDE

GRAYS + BLKS.

SCROLL

WHITE

CONTROL EXPLORATION

14

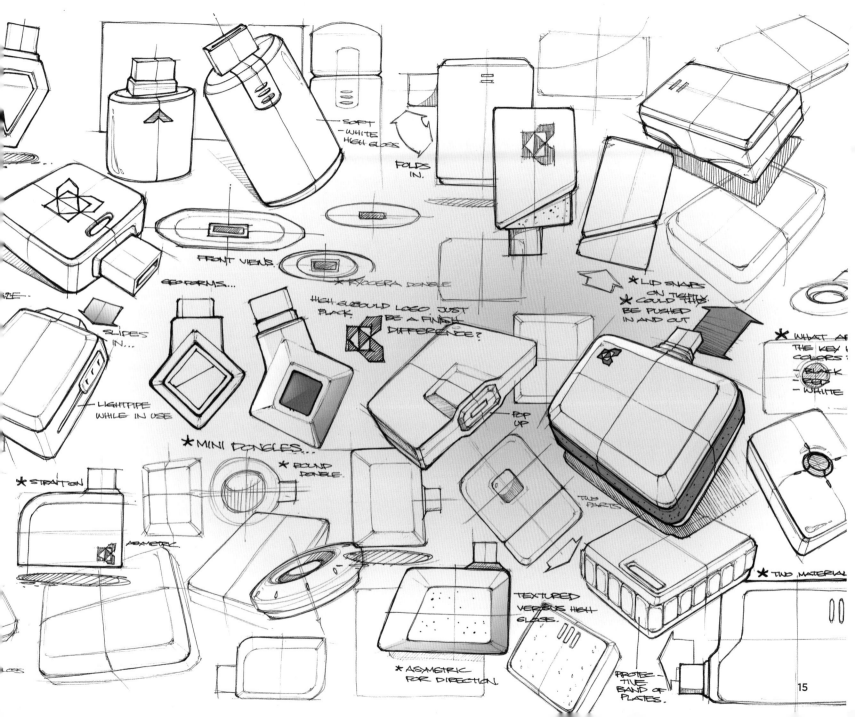

SOFT
- WHITE
HIGH GLOSS

FOLDS
IN.

FRONT VIEWS.

GEO FORMS...

* KYOCERA DONGLE

HIGH GLOSS LOGO, JUST
BLACK

SHOULD LOGO JUST
BE A FINISH
DIFFERENCE?

* LID SNAPS
ON TIGHTLY
* COULD THIS
BE PUSHED
IN AND OUT

* WHAT AR
THE KEY
COLORS
- BLACK
- WHITE

SLIDES
IN...

LIGHTPIPE
WHILE IN USE

* MINI DONGLES...

* ROUND
DONGLE.

POP
UP

TWO
PARTS

* STRATTON

ASYMETRIC.

TEXTURED
VERSUS HIGH
GLOSS.

* TWO MATERIAL

PROTEC-
TIVE
BAND OF
PLATES.

* ASYMETRIC
FOR DIRECTION.

15

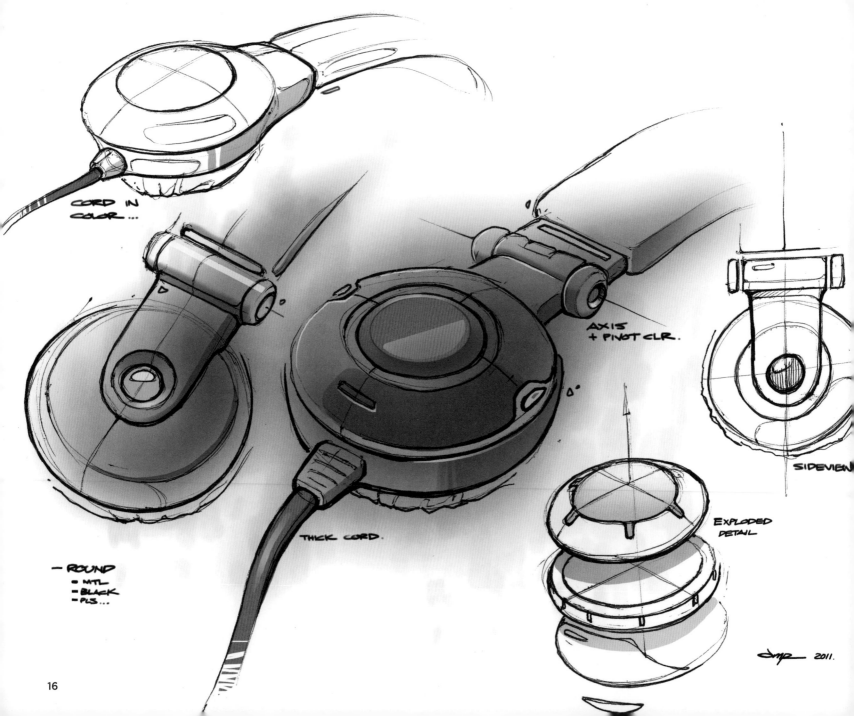

CORD IN
COLOR...

AXIS
+ PIVOT CLR.

SIDEVIEW

THICK CORD.

EXPLODED
DETAIL

- ROUND
  - MTL
  - BLACK
  - PLS...

2011.

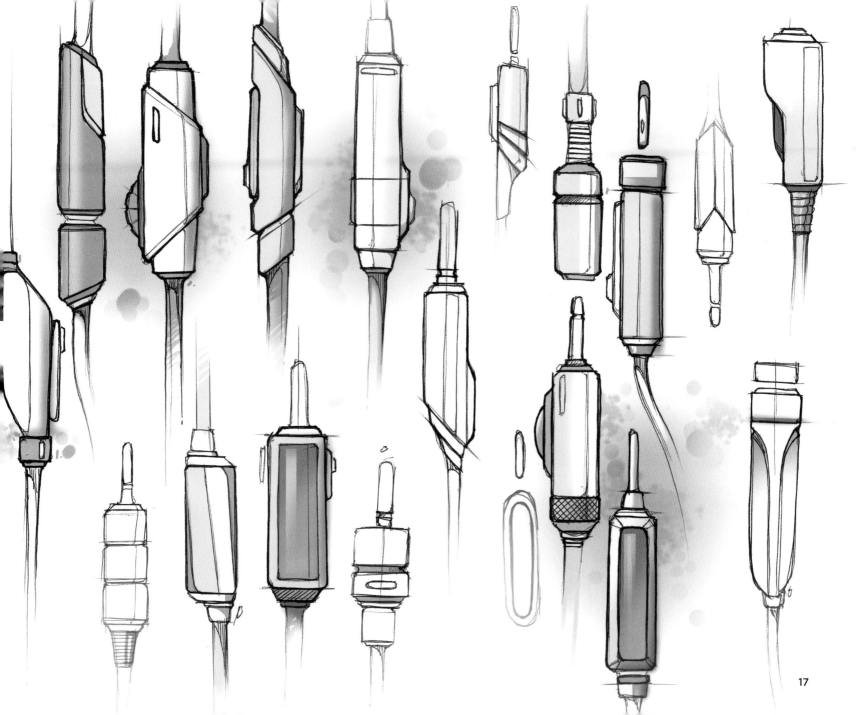

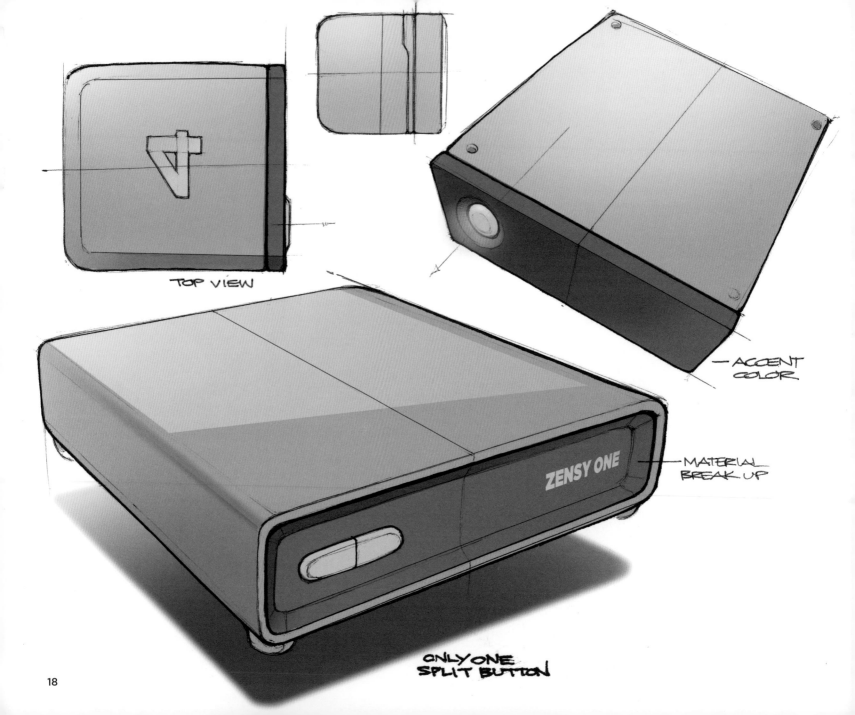

TOP VIEW

ZENSY ONE

ACCENT COLOR

MATERIAL BREAK UP

ONLY ONE SPLIT BUTTON

18

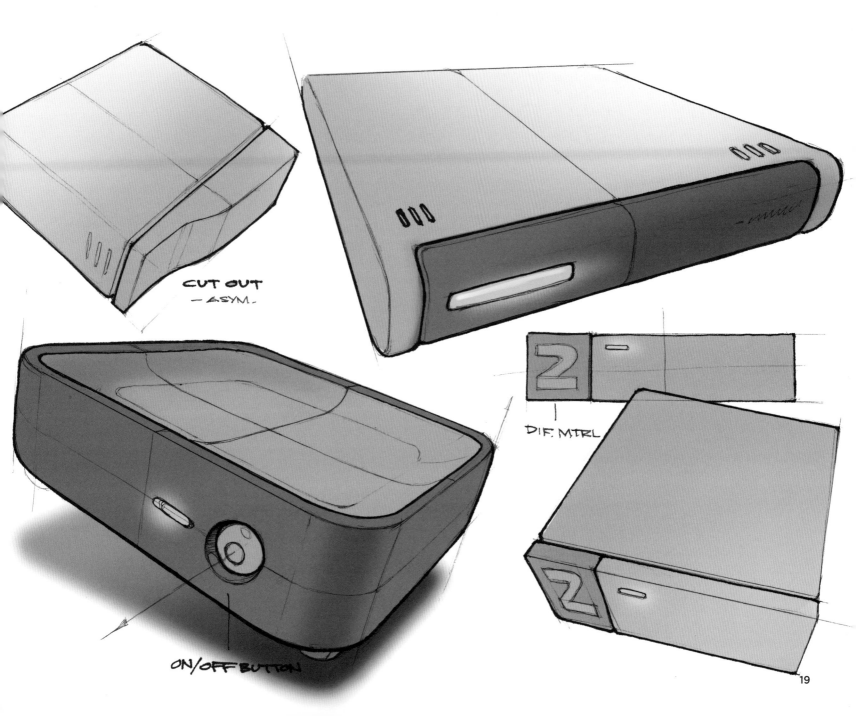

CUT OUT
— ASYM.

DIF. MTRL

ON/OFF BUTTON

19

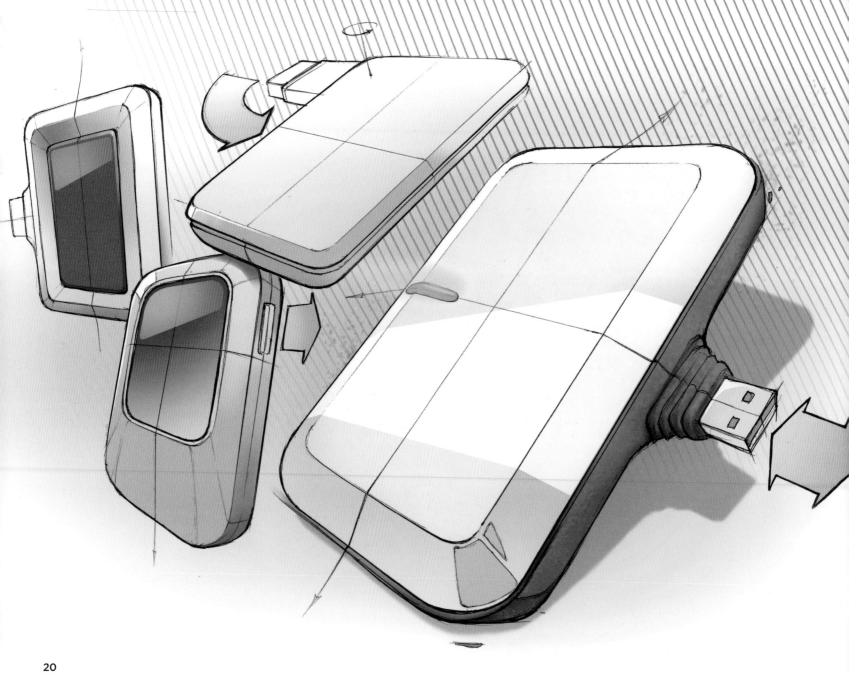

TOP VIEW...

24

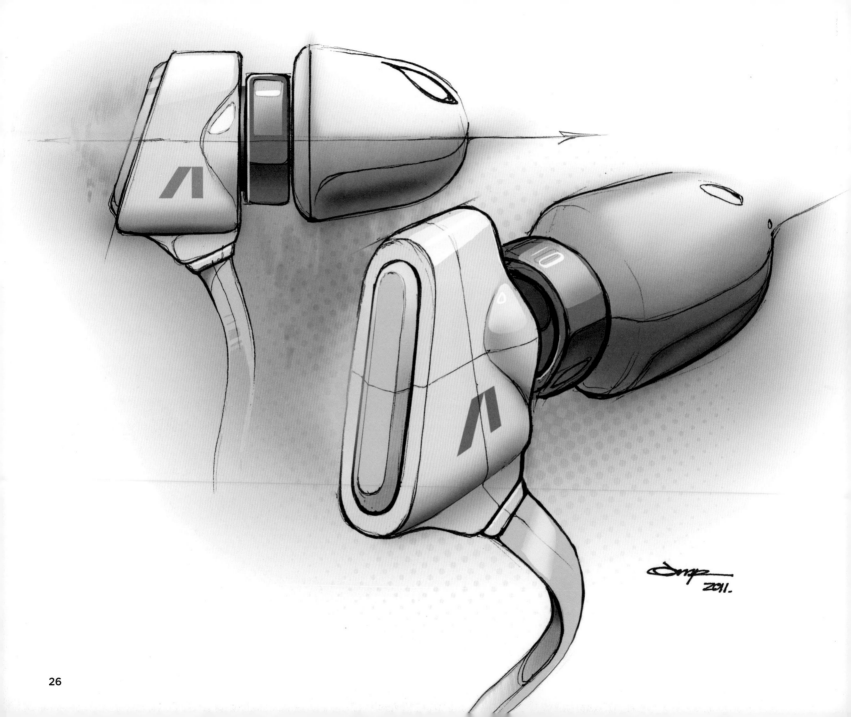

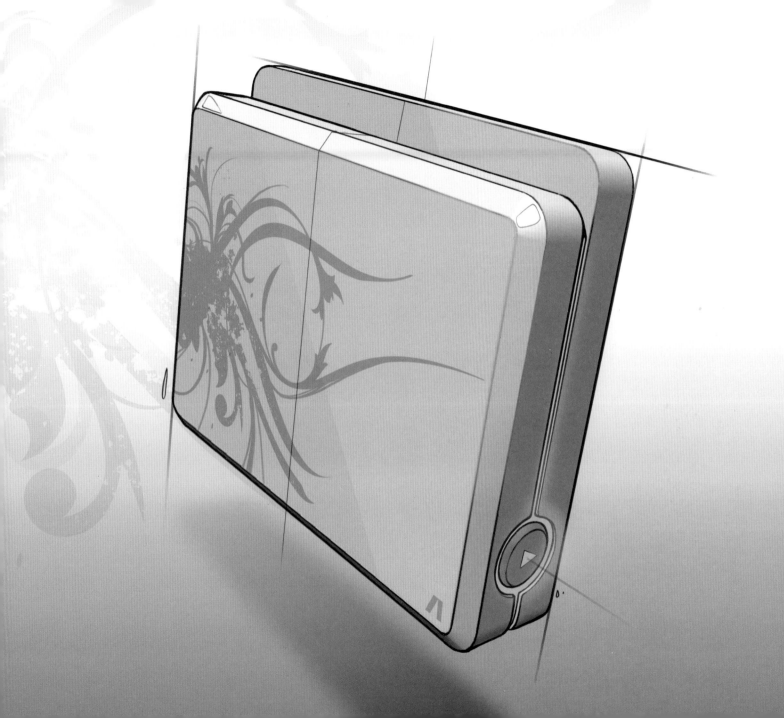

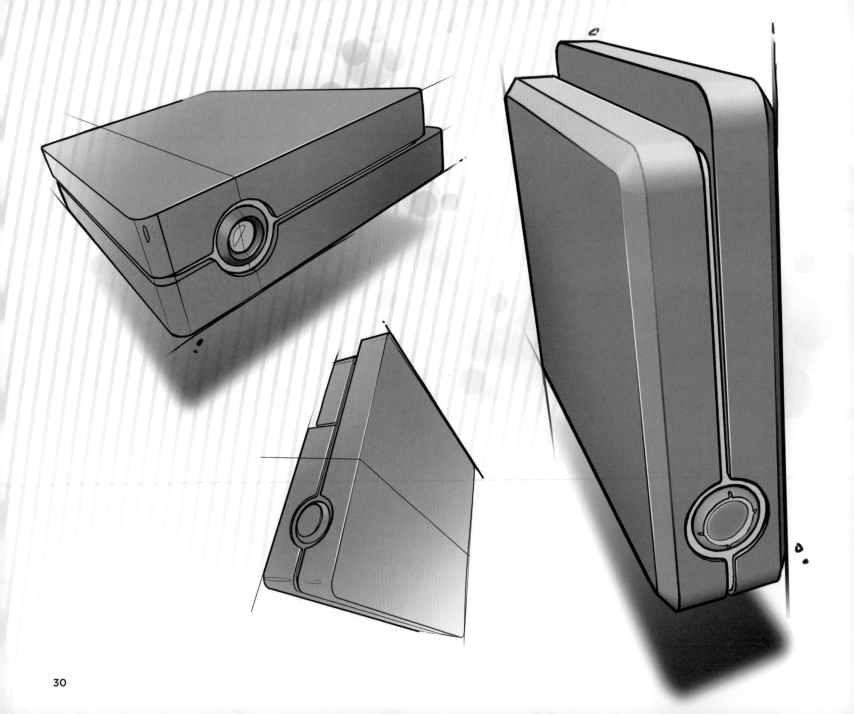

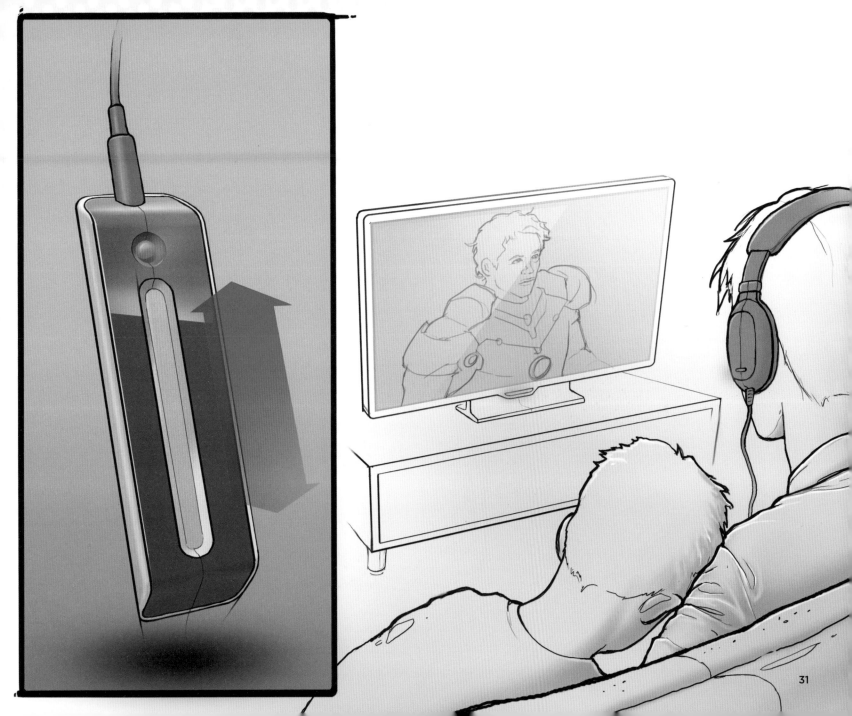

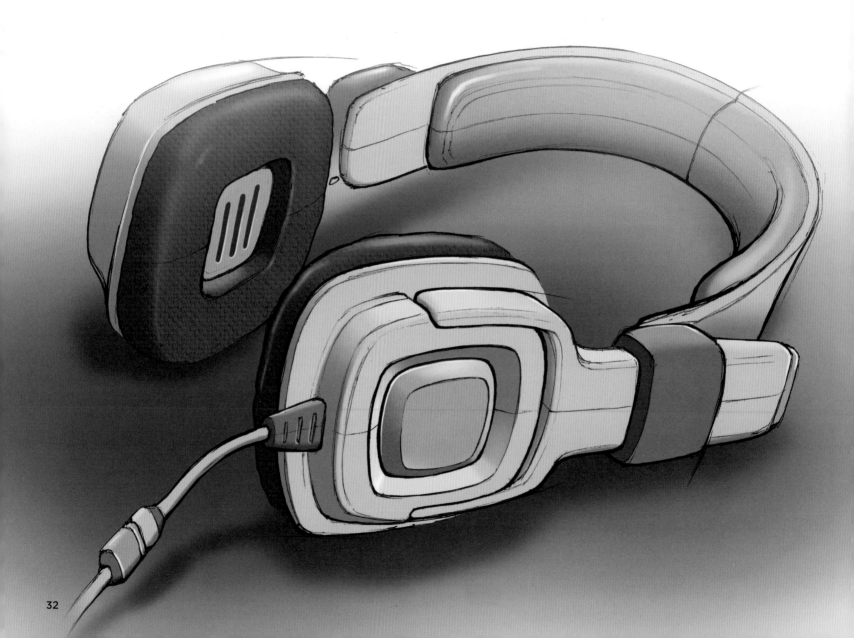

SECTION 2

Watches

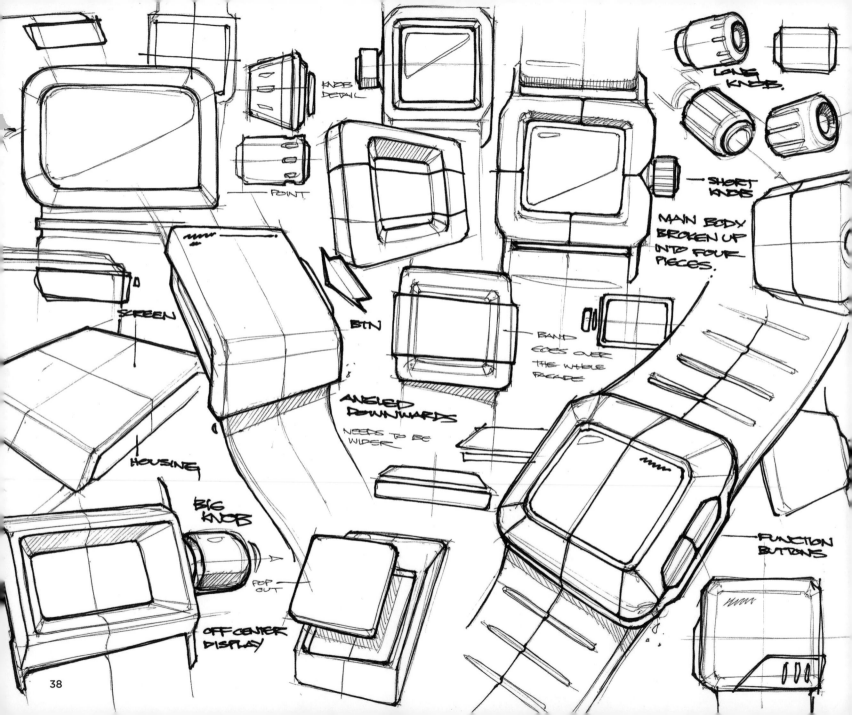

KNOB DETAIL

POINT

LONE KNOBS.

SHORT KNOBS

MAIN BODY BROKEN UP INTO FOUR PIECES.

BTN

BAND GOES OVER THE WHOLE FACADE

SCREEN

ANGLED DOWNWARDS

NEEDS TO BE WIDER

HOUSING

BIG KNOB

POP OUT

OFF CENTER DISPLAY

FUNCTION BUTTONS

38

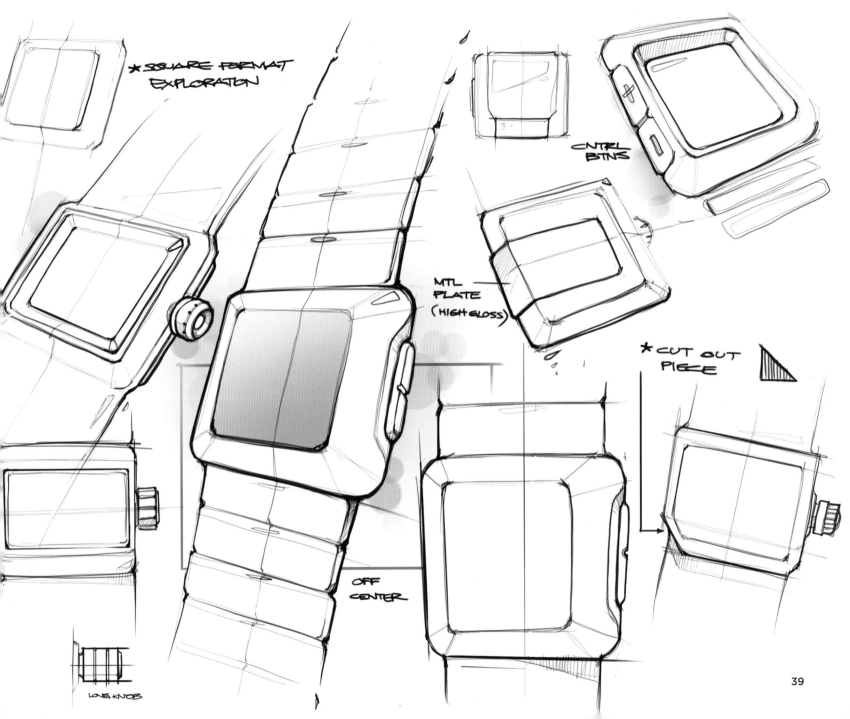

* SQUARE FORMAT EXPLORATION

CNTRL BTNS

MTL PLATE (HIGH GLOSS)

* CUT OUT PIECE

OFF CENTER

LONG KNOB

39

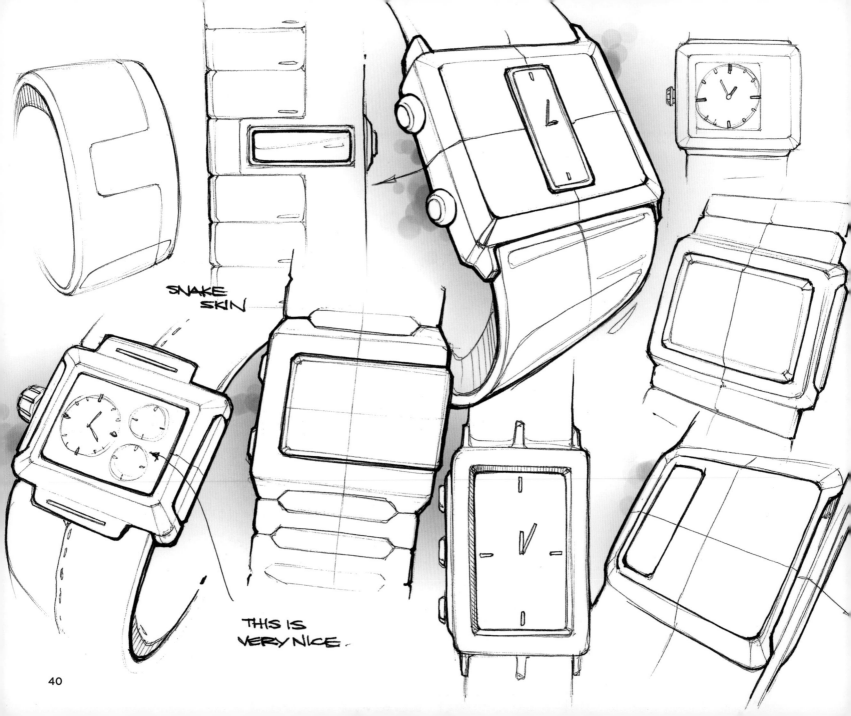

SNAKE
SKIN

THIS IS
VERY NICE.

40

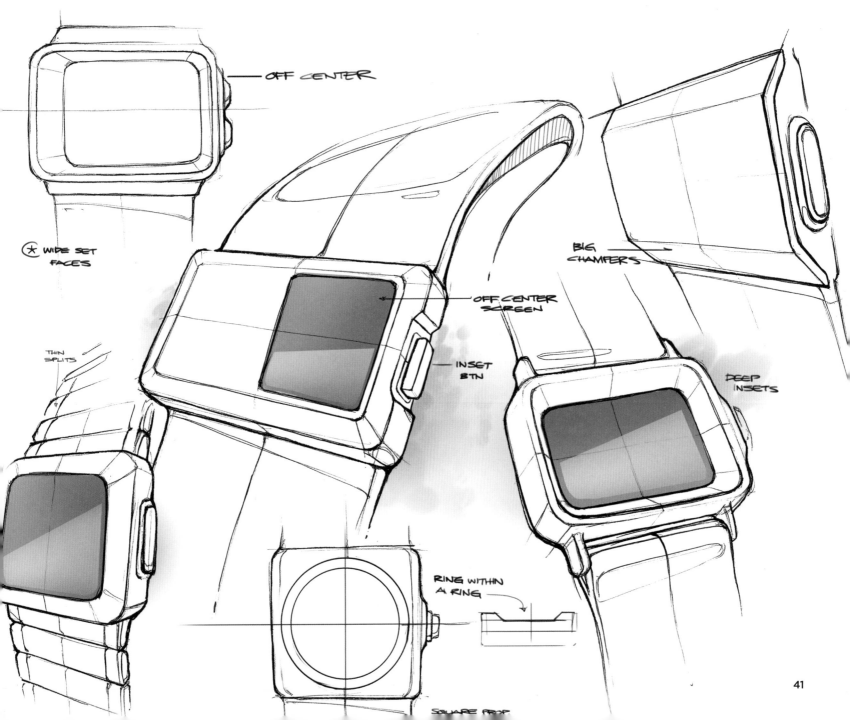

OFF CENTER

★ WIDE SET FACES

THIN SPLITS

BIG CHAMFERS

OFF CENTER SCREEN

INSET BTN

DEEP INSETS

RING WITHIN A RING

SQUARE PROP

41

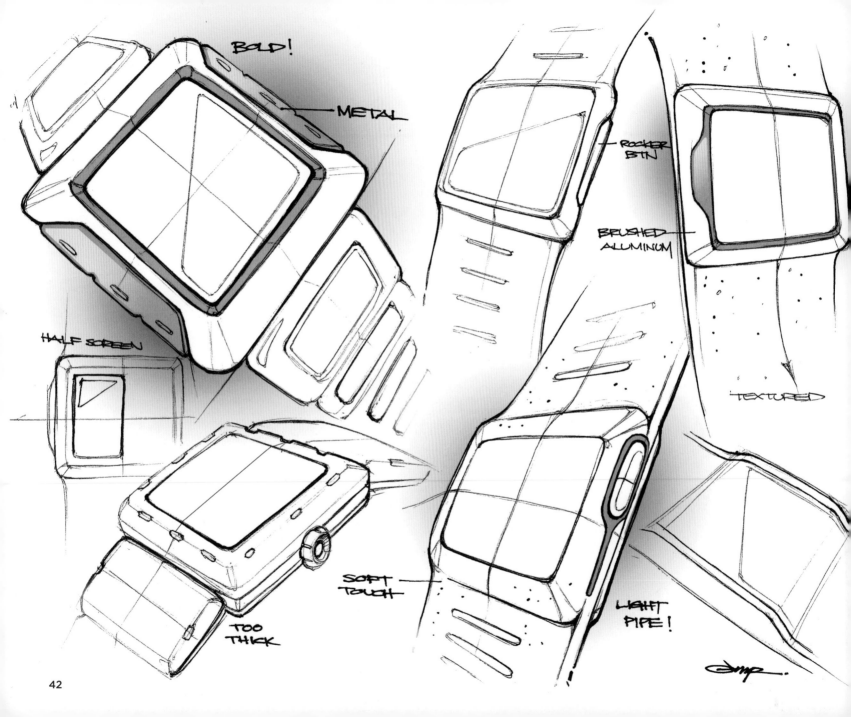

BOLD!

METAL

HALF SCREEN

TOO THICK

ROCKER BTN

BRUSHED ALUMINUM

TEXTURED

SOFT TOUCH

LIGHT PIPE!

42

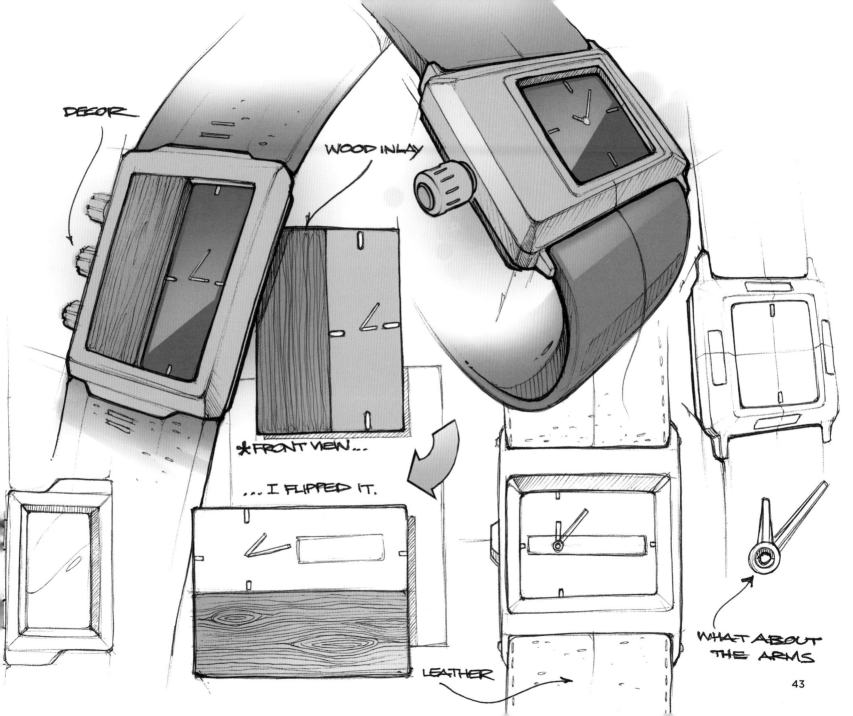

DECOR

WOOD INLAY

*FRONT VIEW...

... I FLIPPED IT.

LEATHER

WHAT ABOUT THE ARMS

43

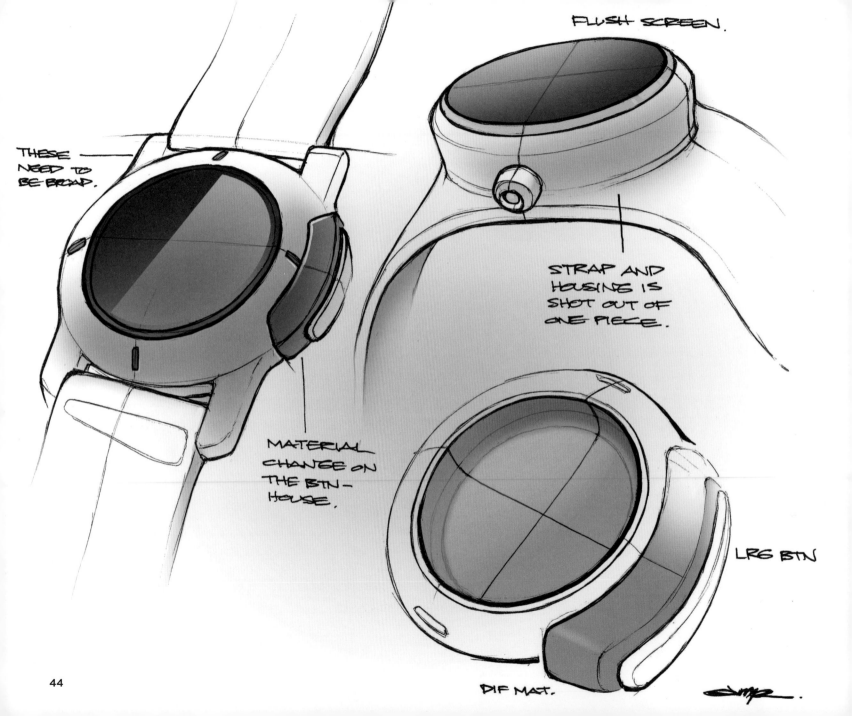

THESE NEED TO BE BROAD.

FLUSH SCREEN.

STRAP AND HOUSING IS SHOT OUT OF ONE PIECE.

MATERIAL CHANGE ON THE BTN-HOUSE.

LRG BTN

DIF MAT.

44

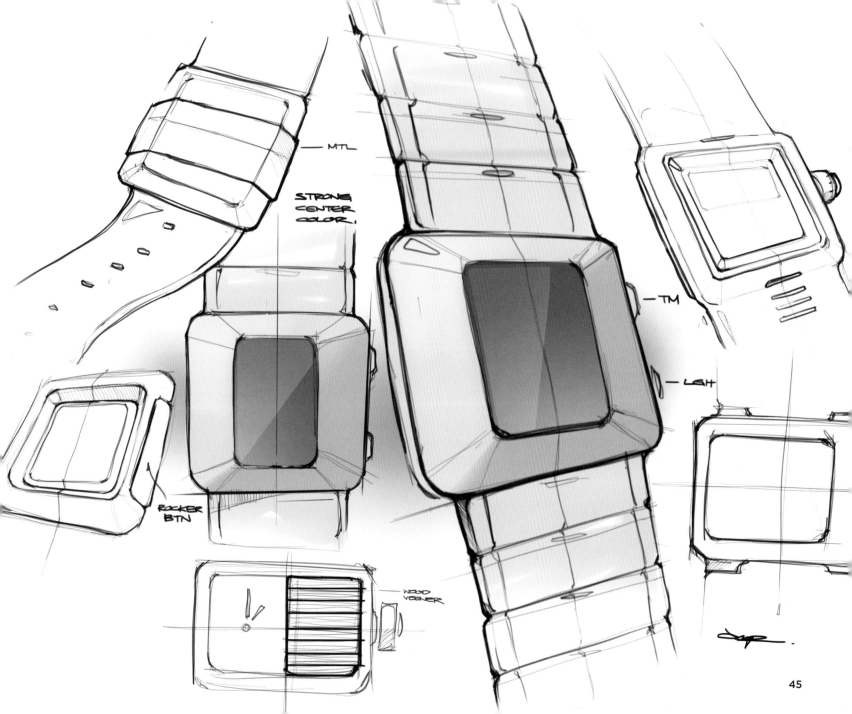

MTL

STRONG
CENTER
COLOR

TM

LGH

ROCKER
BTN

WOOD
VENEER

45

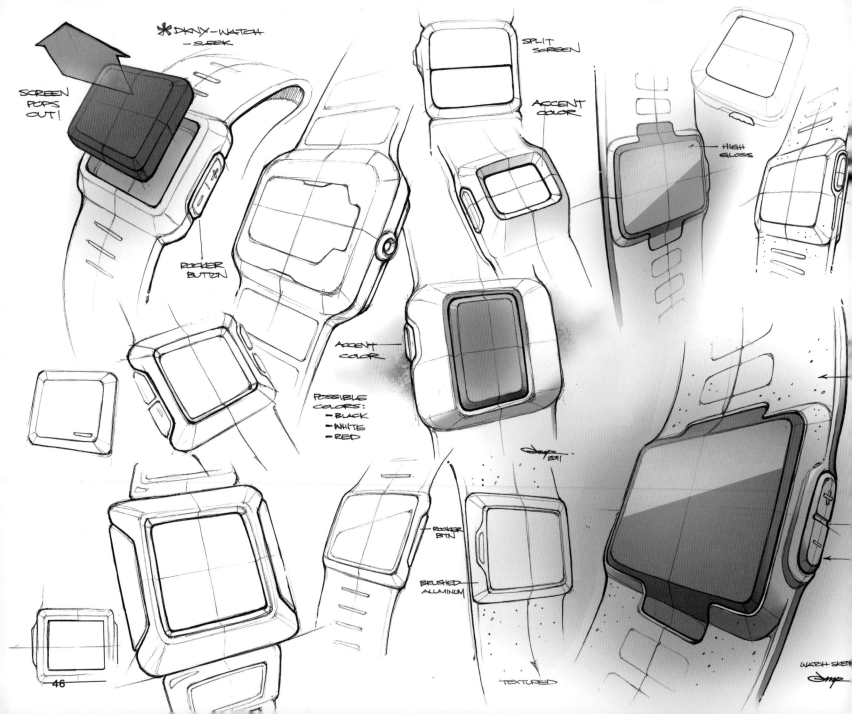

✳ DKNY-WATCH
  - SLEEK

SCREEN
POPS
OUT!

ROCKER
BUTTON

ACCENT
COLOR

POSSIBLE
COLORS:
- BLACK
- WHITE
- RED

SPLIT
SCREEN

ACCENT
COLOR

HIGH
GLOSS

ROCKER
BTN

BRUSHED
ALUMINUM

TEXTURED

WATCH SKE

46

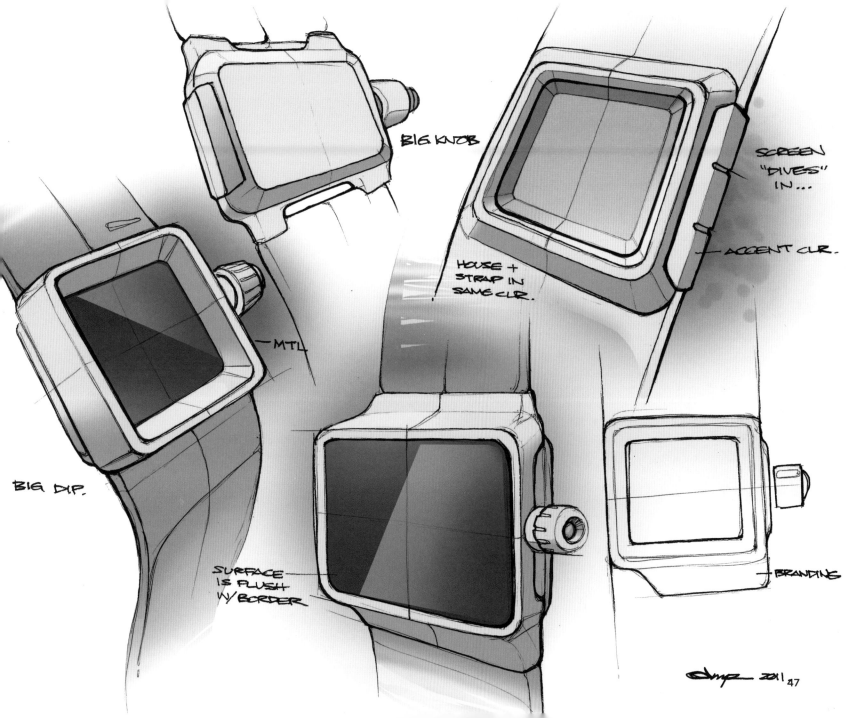

BIG KNOB

SCREEN "DIVES" IN...

ACCENT CLR.

HOUSE + STRAP IN SAME CLR.

MTL

BIG DIP.

SURFACE IS FLUSH W/ BORDER

BRANDING

2011 47

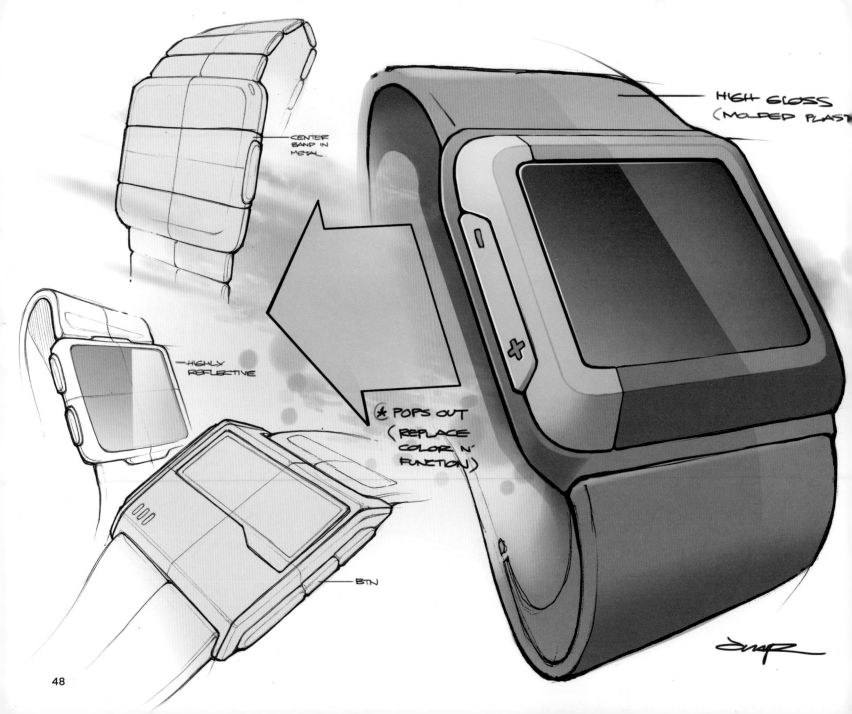

CENTER BAND IN METAL.

HIGH GLOSS (MOLDED PLAST

HIGHLY REFLECTIVE

(*) POPS OUT (REPLACE COLOR N' FUNCTION)

BTN

48

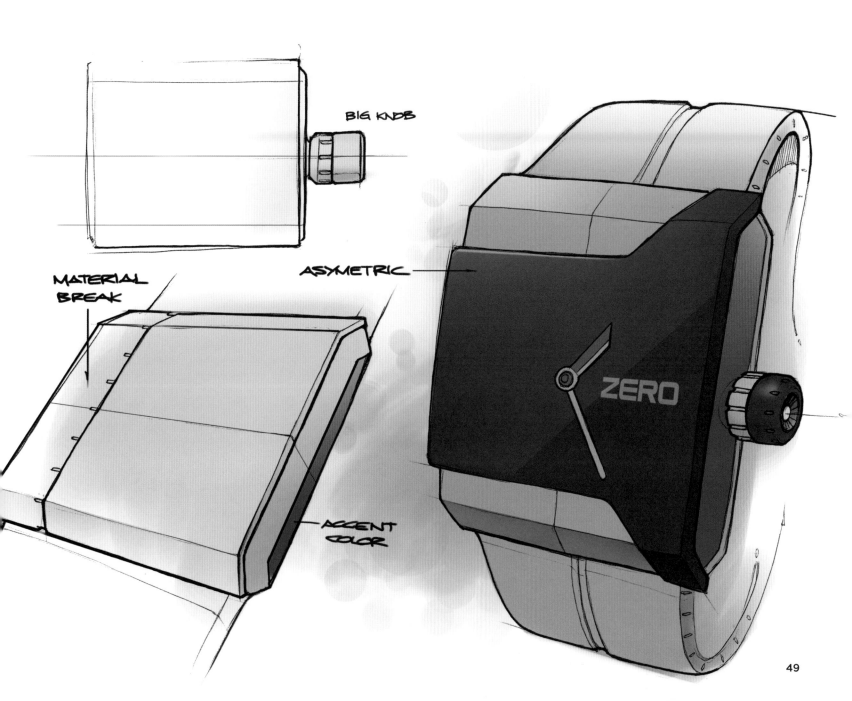

BIG KNOB

MATERIAL BREAK

ASYMETRIC

ACCENT COLOR

ZERO

49

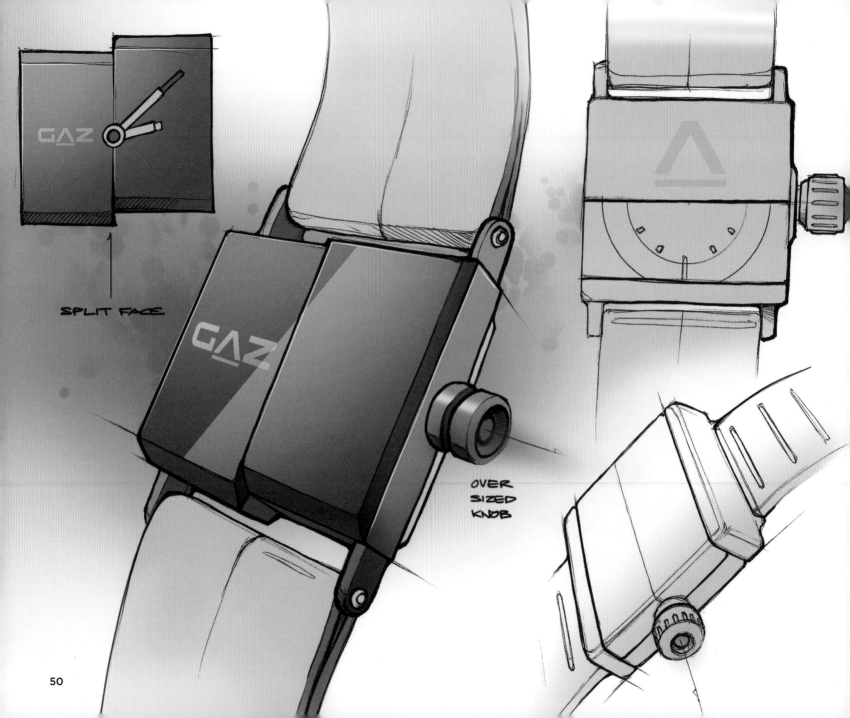

SPLIT FACE

GAZ

OVER SIZED KNOB

50

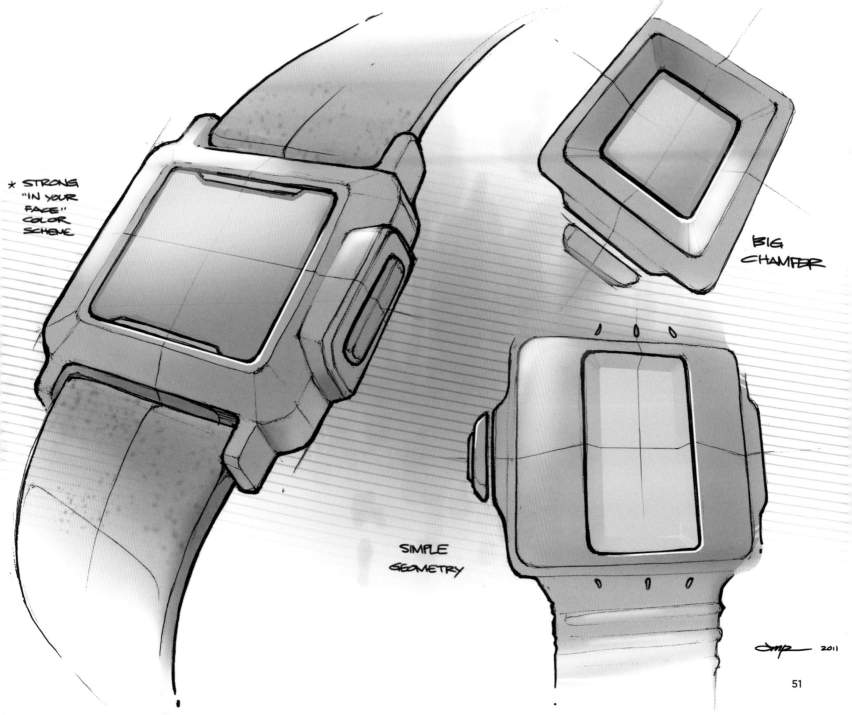

* STRONG "IN YOUR FACE" COLOR SCHEME

BIG CHAMFER

SIMPLE GEOMETRY

2011

51

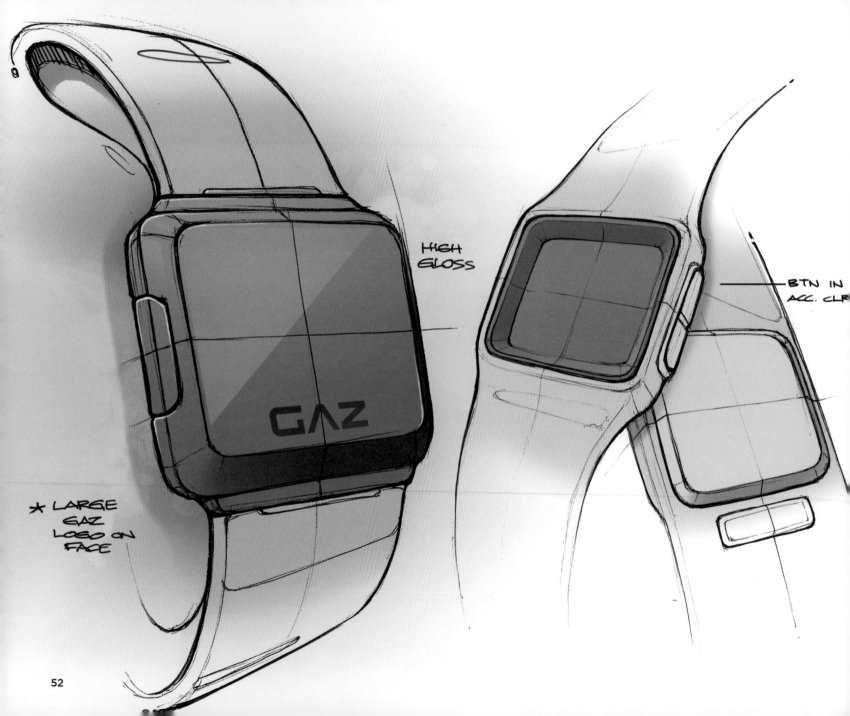

HIGH
GLOSS

BTN IN
ACC. CLR

★ LARGE
GAZ
LOGO ON
FACE

GAZ

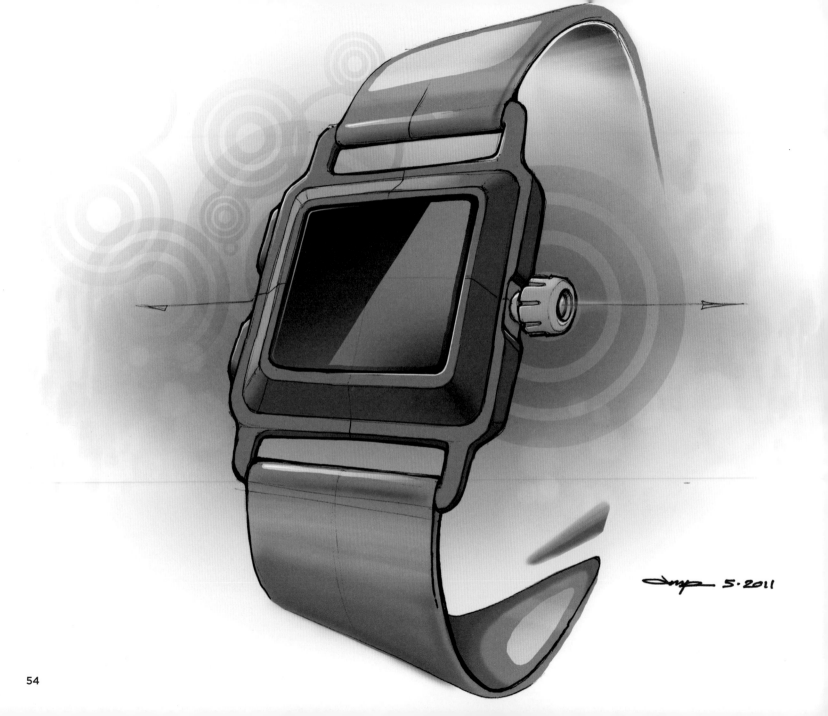

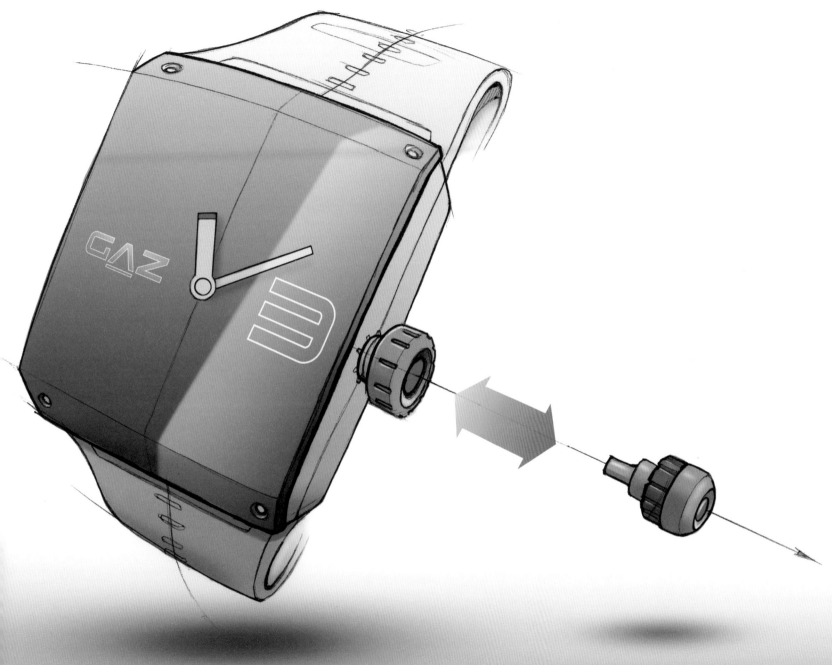

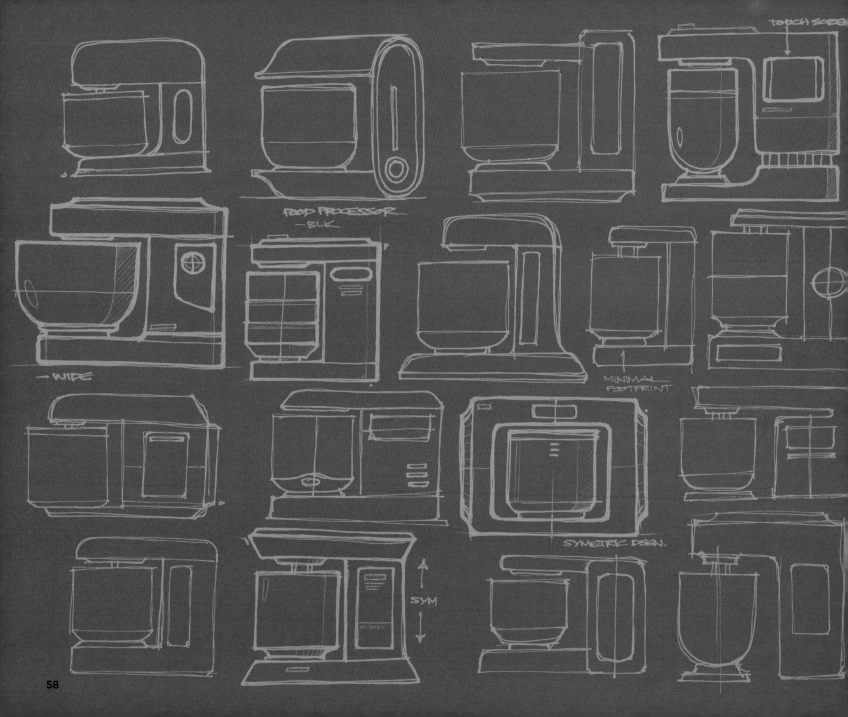

TOUCH SCREEN

FOOD PROCESSOR
—BLK

—WIDE

MINIMAL
FOOTPRINT

SYMETRIC DSGN.

SYM

58

COFFEE MAKER

SECTION 3
home appliances

HOUR GLASS

THICK EDGE

BROAD BASE

MTL

MTL

— WRK W/ THS

SPLIT MTRL

LONG & THIN.

ASYMETRK

*WHAT ABOUT MATERIALS?
- STAINLESS
- 60 GLASS
- ACC CLR

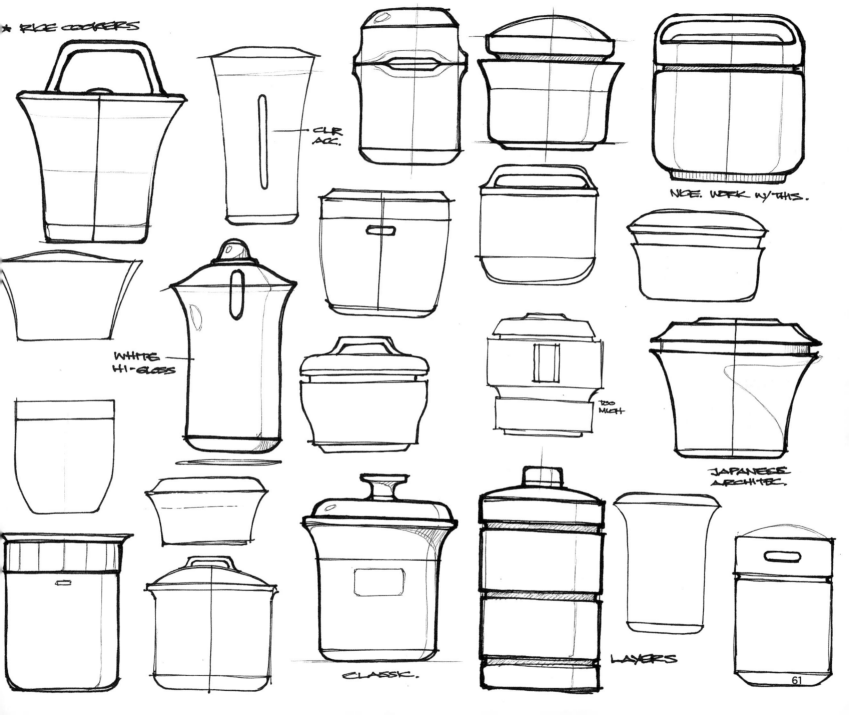

* RICE COOKERS

CLR
ACC.

NICE. WORK W/ THIS.

WHITE
HI-GLOSS

TOO
MUCH

JAPANESE
ARCHITEC.

CLASSIC.

LAYERS

61

DIAGNAL SLICE.

BULKY

BROAD BEE.

ACCENT COLOR

FAST

62

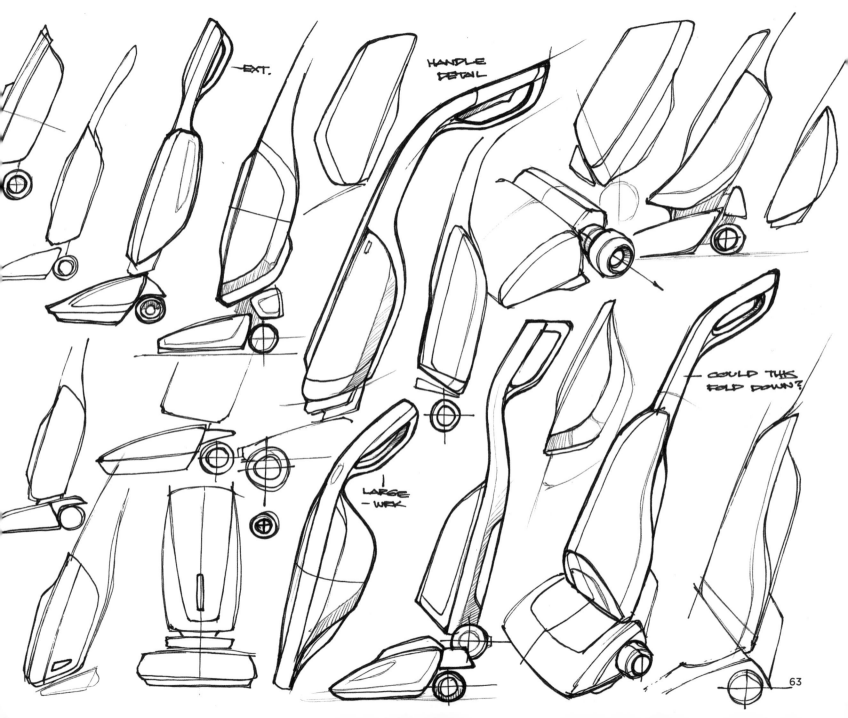

EXT.

HANDLE
DETAIL

COULD THIS
FOLD DOWN?

LARGE
- WRK

63

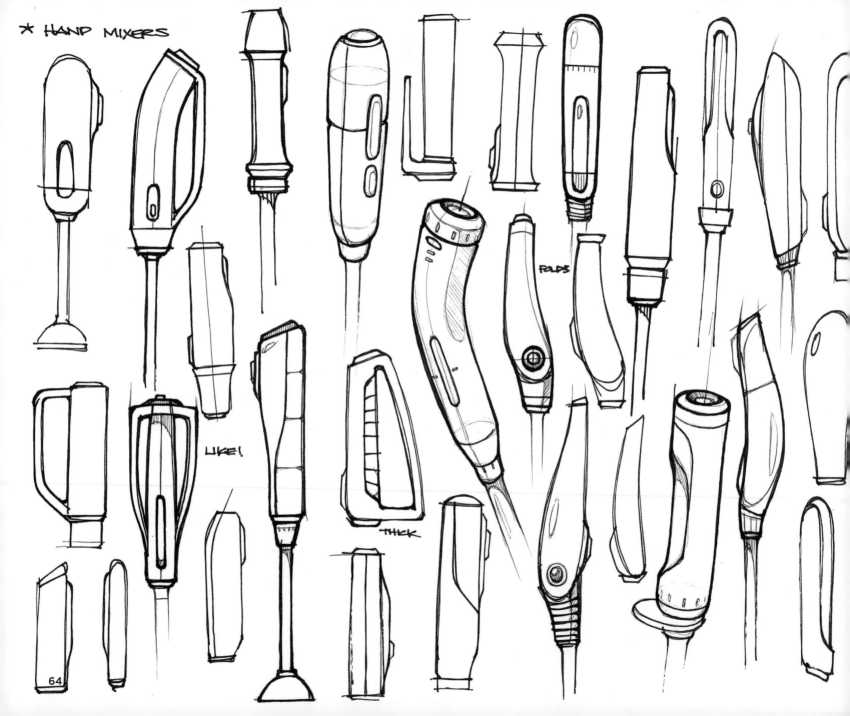

* HAND MIXERS

FOLDS

LIKE!

THICK

64

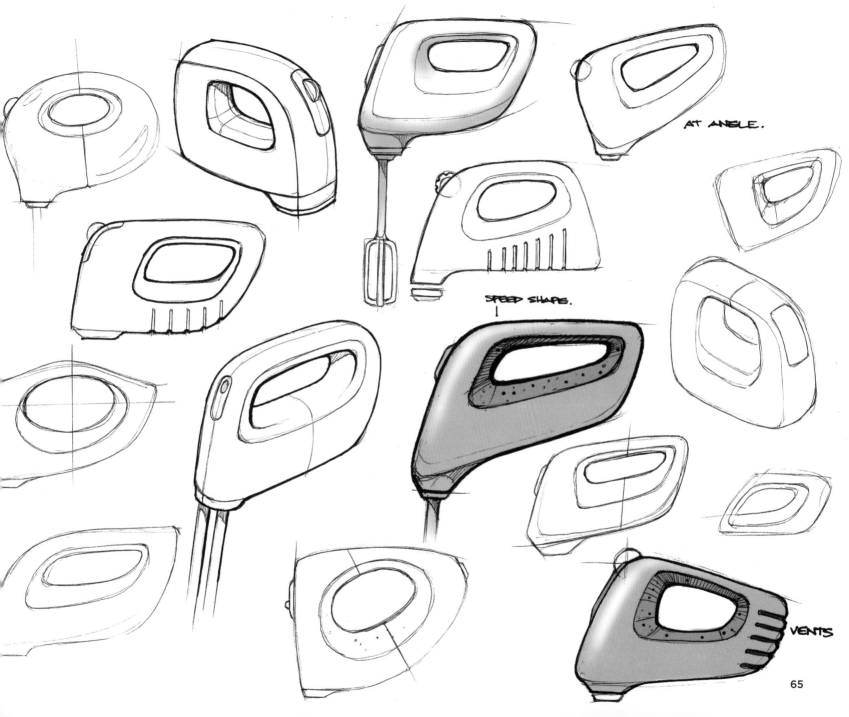

AT ANGLE.

SPEED SHAPE.

VENTS

65

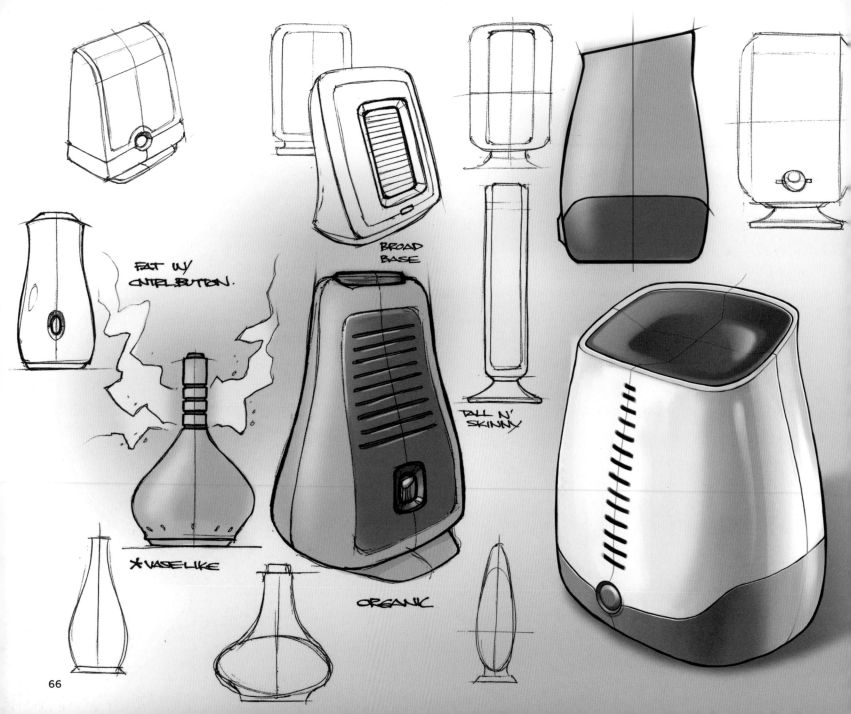

FAT W/
CNTRL BUTTON.

BROAD
BASE

*VASELIKE

ORGANIC

TALL N'
SKINNY

TOASTER
- CIRCLE BASED
- SLIDER
- CIRCULAR PEG.
- 3 MAT.

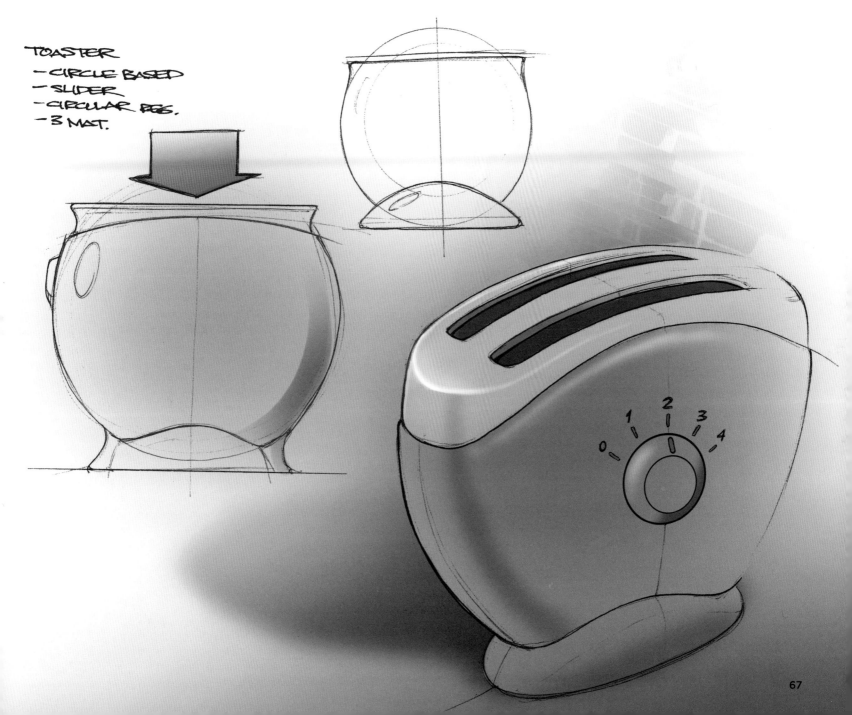

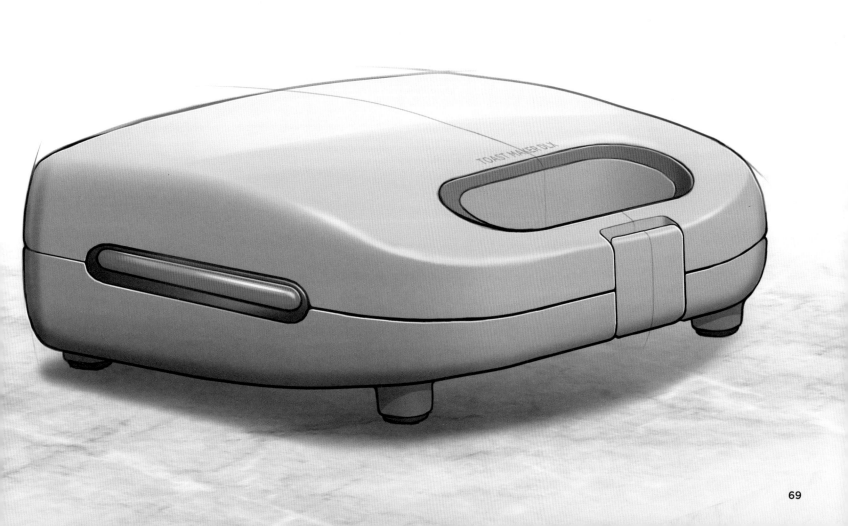

TOAST MAKER D.X

PIZZA DOUGH

PHASE 1

PHASE 2

-Kneading
-4min

PHASE 3

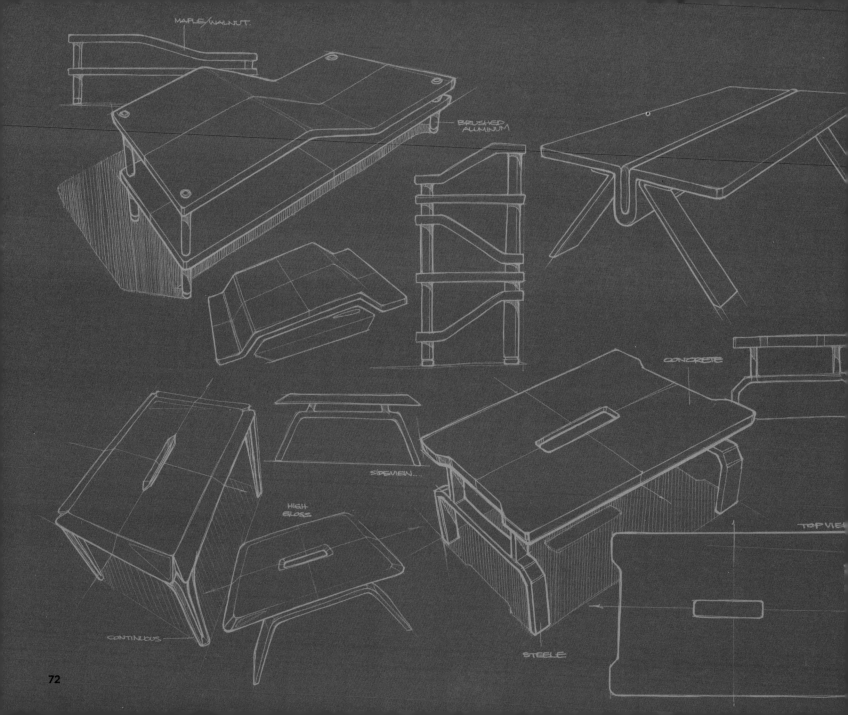

MAPLE/WALNUT.

BRUSHED ALUMINUM

CONCRETE

SIDEVIEW...

HIGH GLOSS

TOP VIEW

STEELE

CONTINUOUS

72

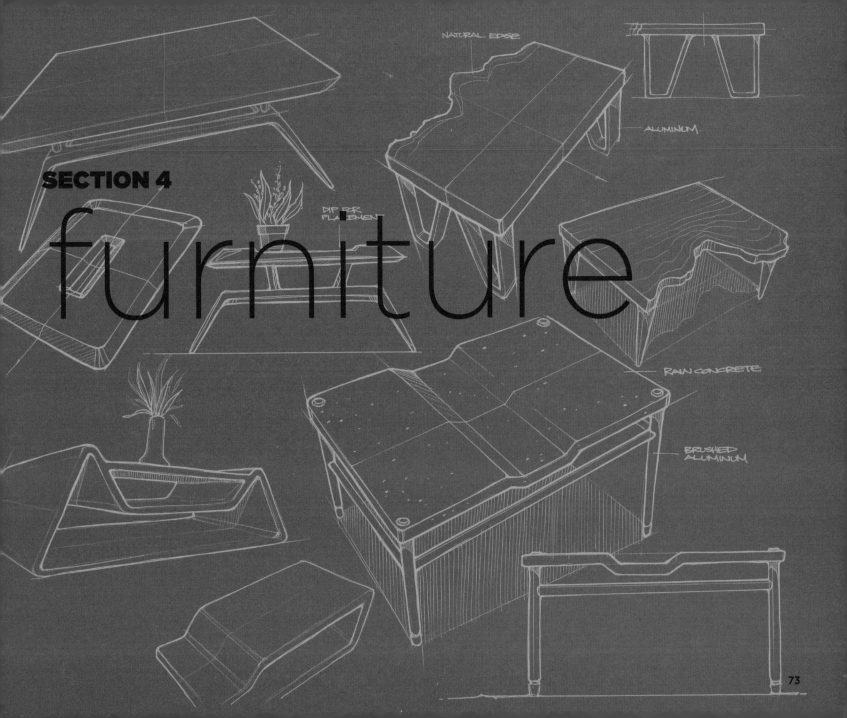

SECTION 4

furniture

NATURAL EDGE

ALUMINUM

DIP PER PLACEMENT

RAW CONCRETE

BRUSHED ALUMINUM

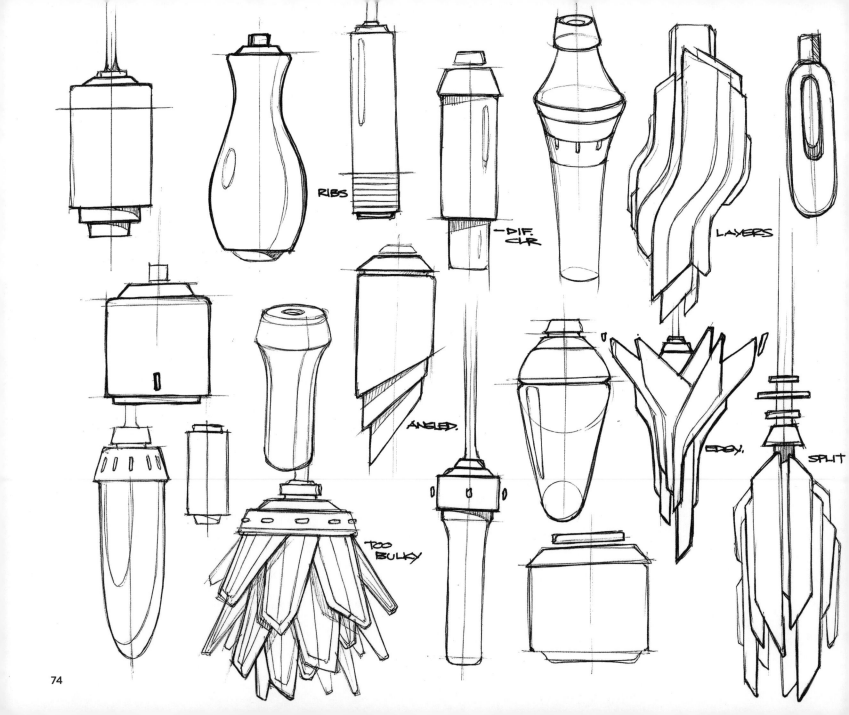

RIBS

DIF. CLR

LAYERS

ANGLED.

TOO BULKY

EDDY.

SPLIT

74

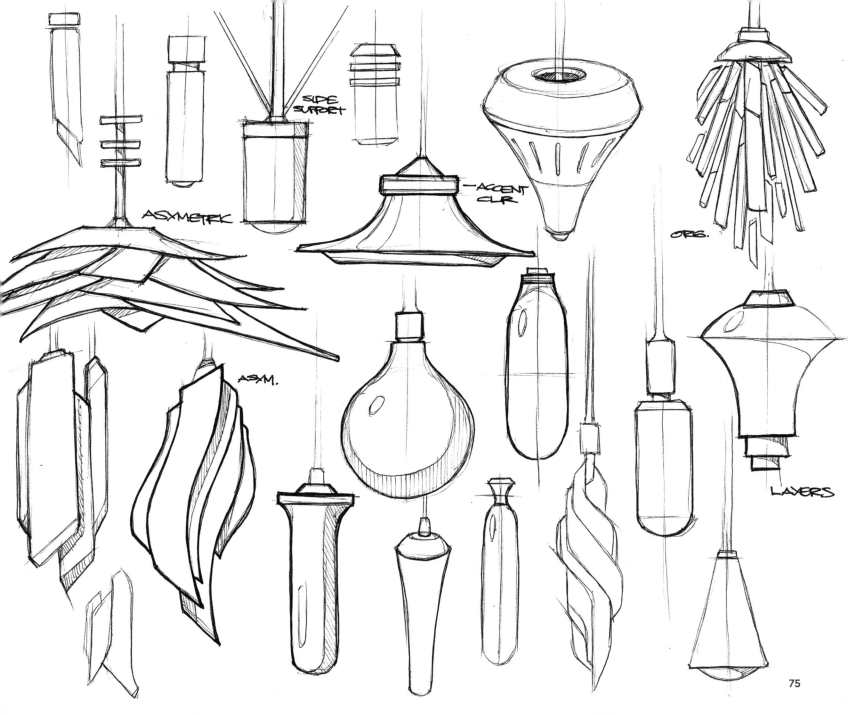

SIDE
SUPPORT

ASYMETRK

ASM.

—ACCENT
CLR

ORG.

LAYERS

75

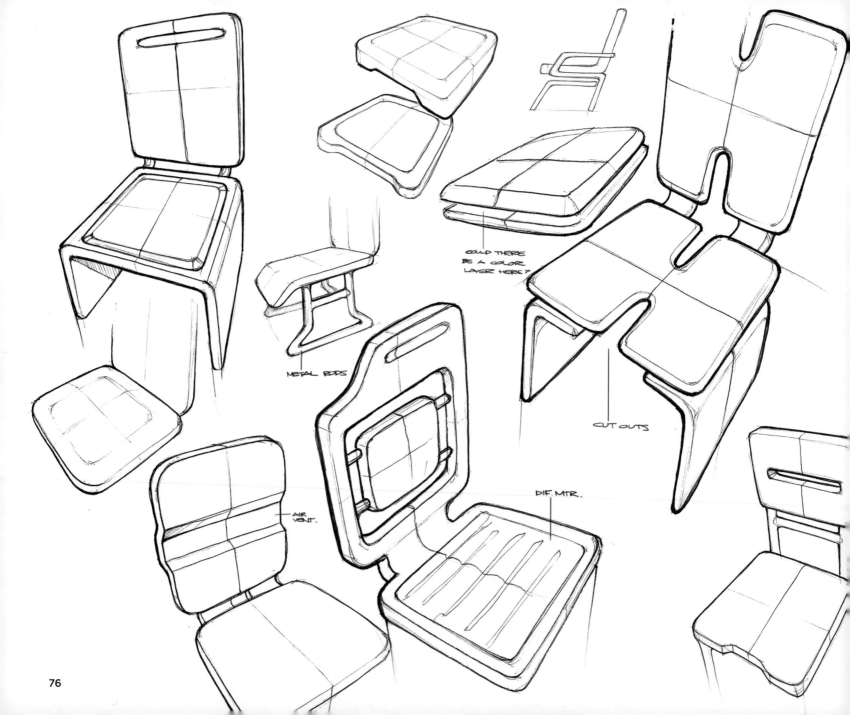

COULD THERE BE A COLOR LAYER HERE?

METAL RODS

CUT OUTS

AIR VENT.

DIF. MTR.

76

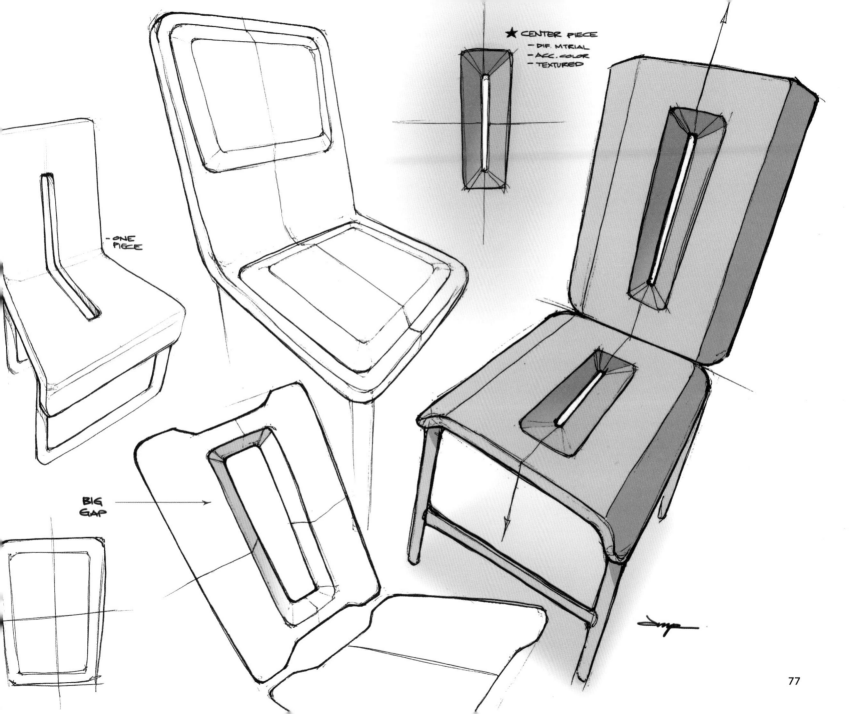

★ CENTER PIECE
- DIF. M'TRIAL
- ACC. COLOR
- TEXTURED

- ONE PIECE

BIG GAP

77

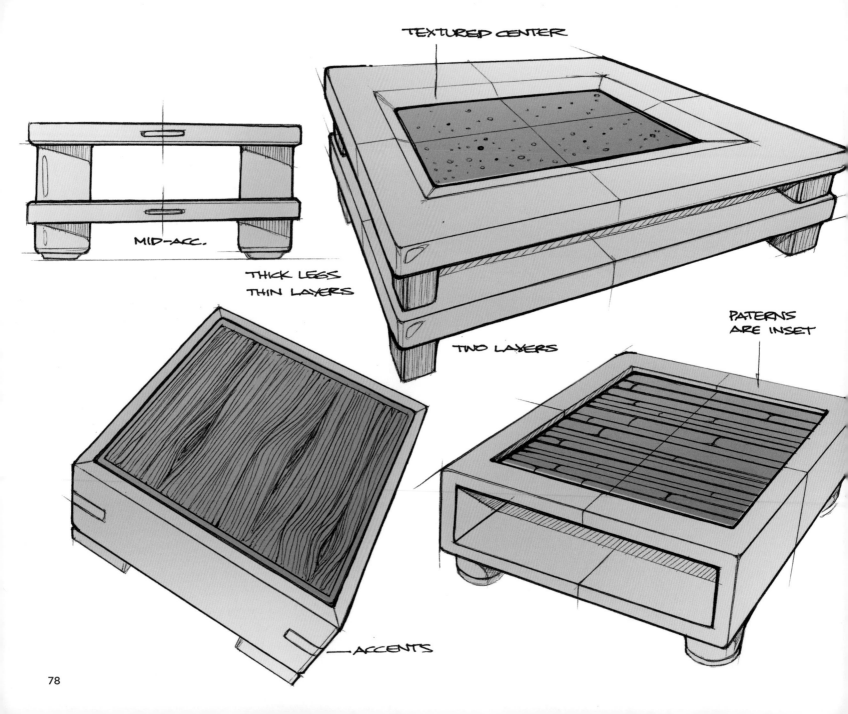

TEXTURED CENTER

MID-ACC.

THICK LEGS
THIN LAYERS

TWO LAYERS

PATERNS
ARE INSET

ACCENTS

78

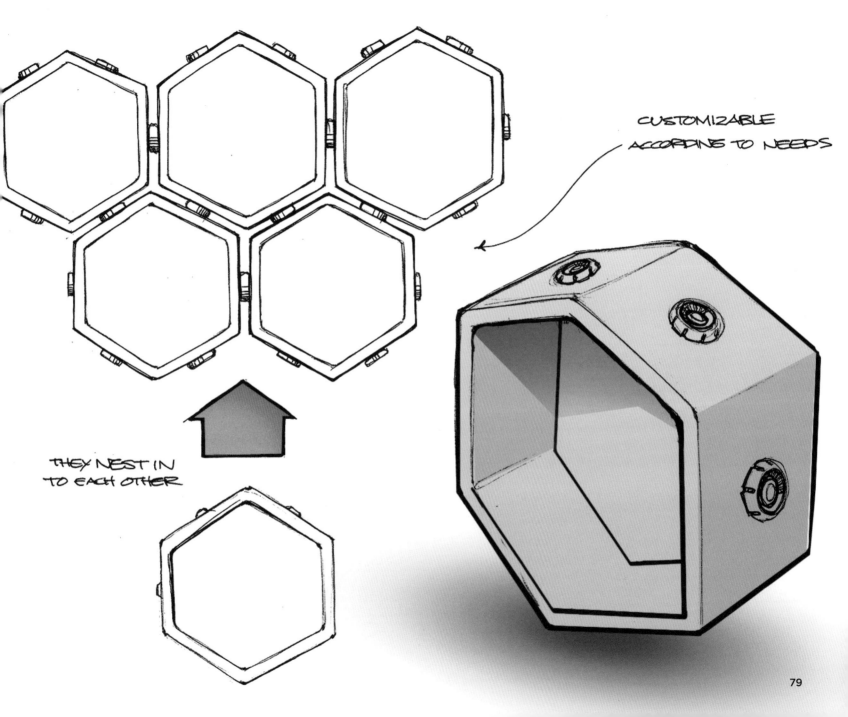

CUSTOMIZABLE
ACCORDING TO NEEDS

THEY NEST IN
TO EACH OTHER

79

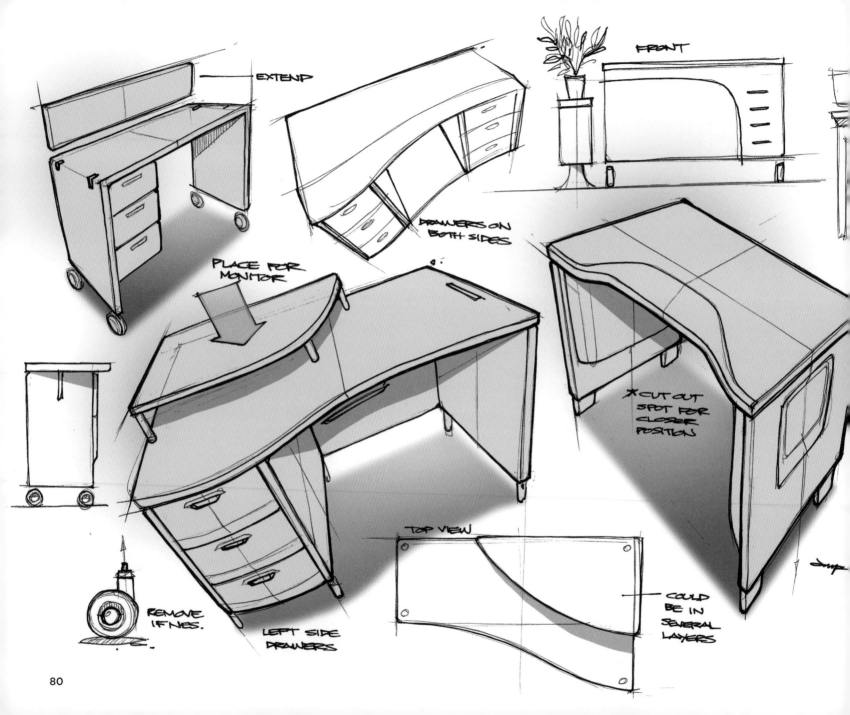

EXTEND

FRONT

DRAWERS ON
BOTH SIDES

PLACE FOR
MONITOR

*CUT OUT
SPOT FOR
CLOSER
POSITION

REMOVE
IF NES.

LEFT SIDE
DRAWERS

TOP VIEW

COULD
BE IN
SEVERAL
LAYERS

80

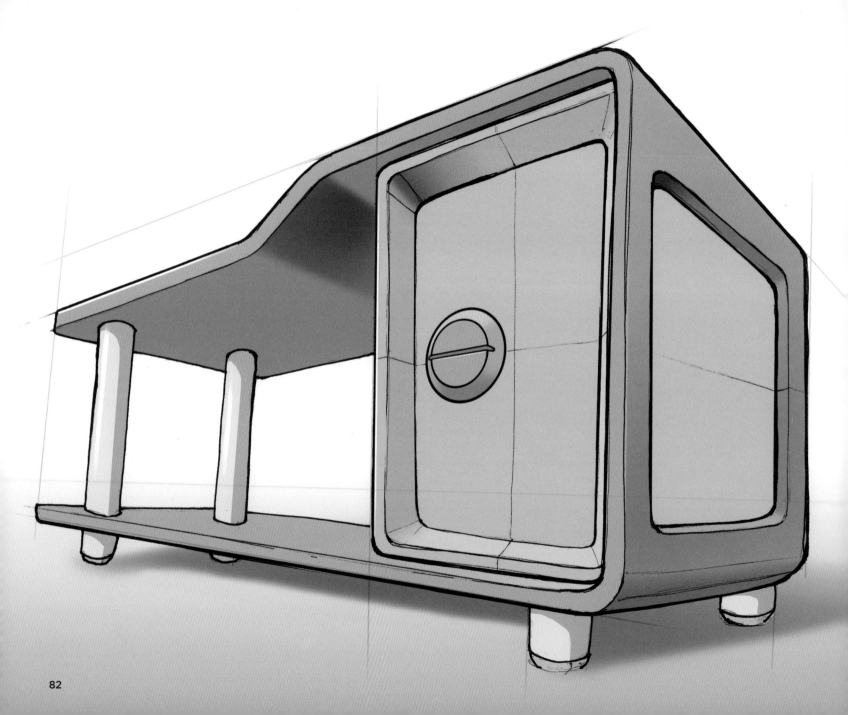

83

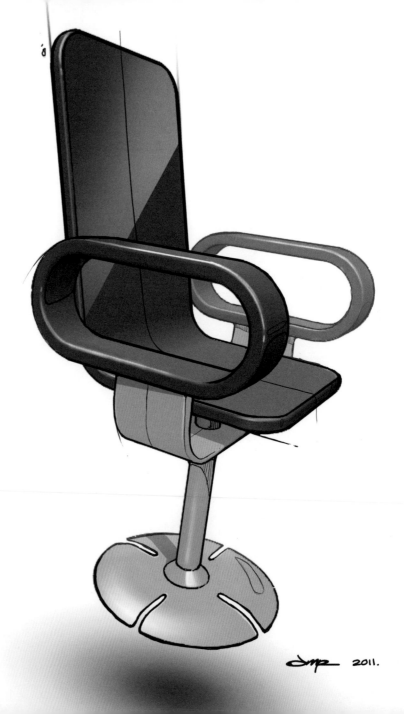

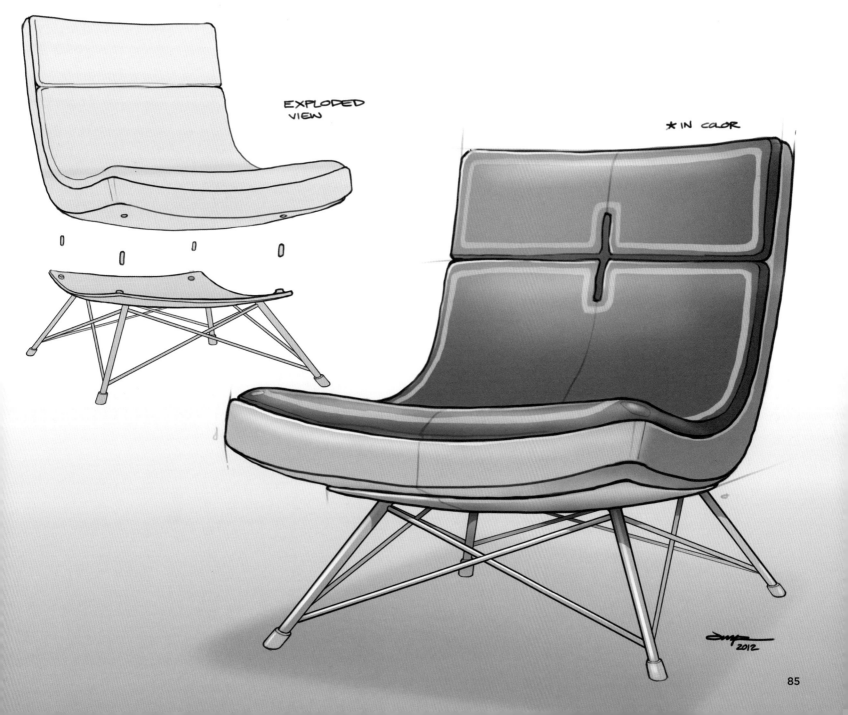

EXPLODED
VIEW

* IN COLOR

2012

85

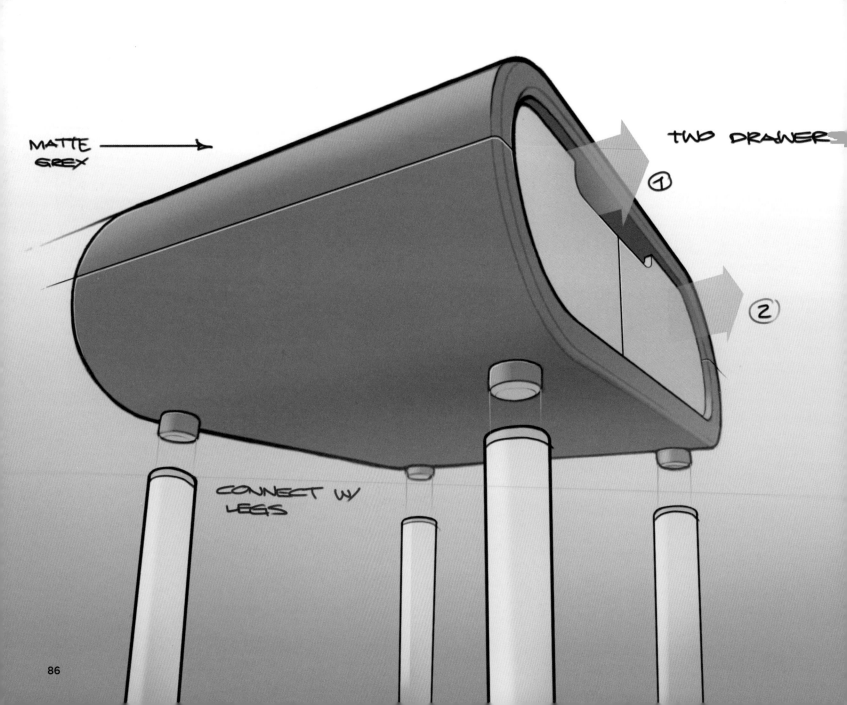

MATTE GREX

TWO DRAWER

① ②

CONNECT W LEGS

I LIKE THE ANGEL
OF THE GAS TANK

THICK TO
THIN

TOO FUTURISTIC

BATTERY (TOO BULKY)

88

SECTION 5

mobility

89

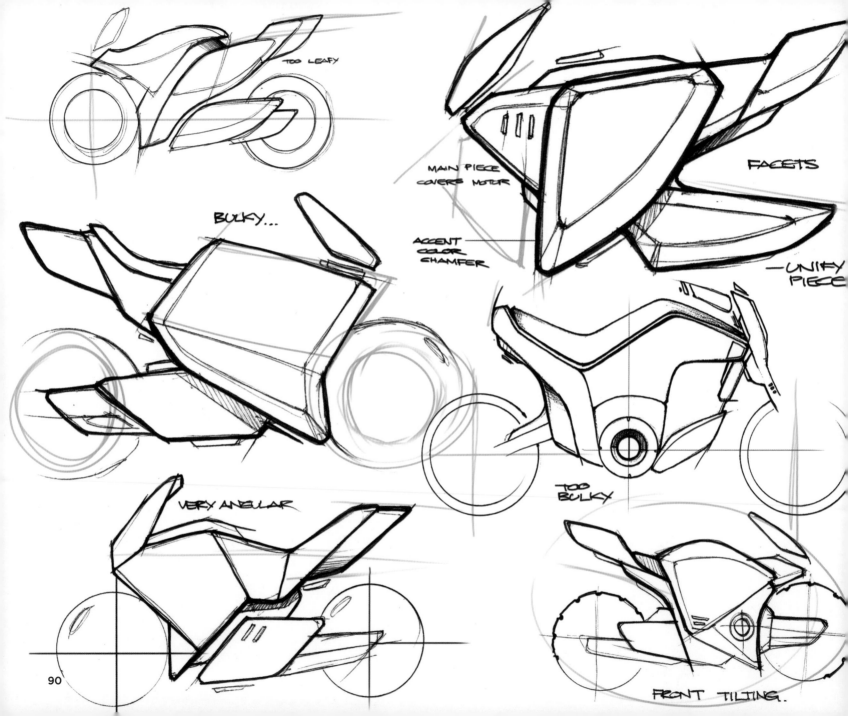

TOO LEAFY

MAIN PIECE
COVERS MOTOR

FACETS

ACCENT
COLOR
CHAMFER

UNIFY
PIECE

BULKY...

VERY ANGULAR

TOO
BULKY

FRONT TILTING.

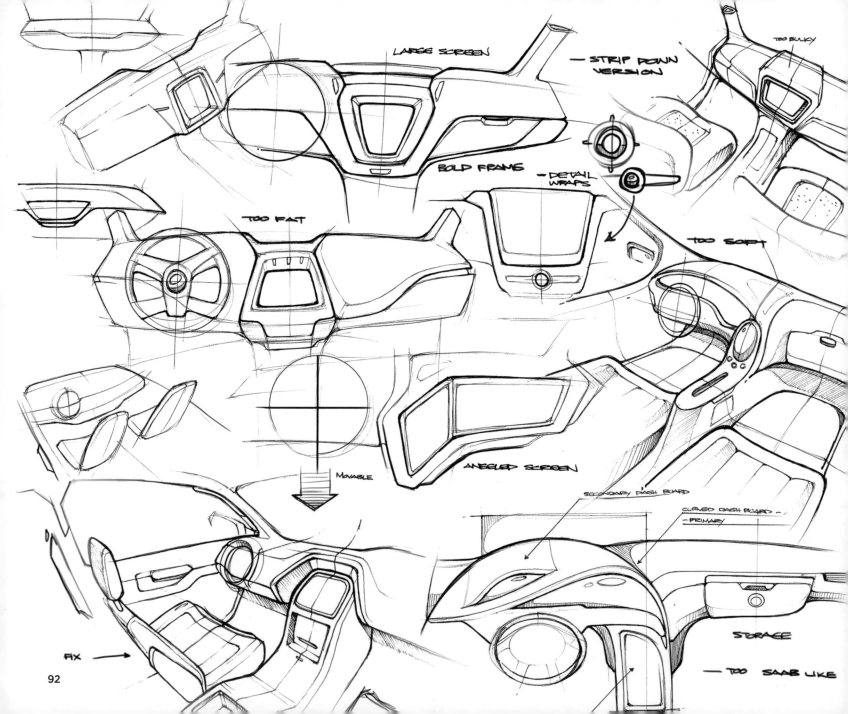

LARGE SCREEN

— STRIP DOWN
VERSION

TOO BULKY

BOLD FRAME

— DETAIL
WRAPS

TOO FAT

TOO SOFT

ANGLED SCREEN

MOVABLE

SECONDARY DASH BOARD

CURVED DASH BOARD —
— PRIMARY

FIX →

STORAGE

— TOO SAAB LIKE

92

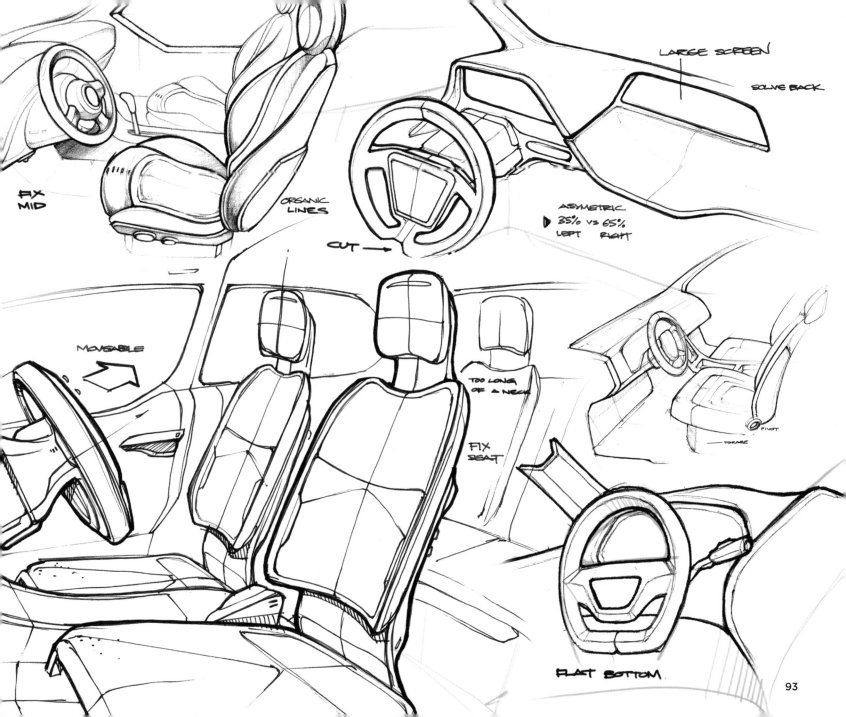

FIX MID

ORGANIC LINES

CUT →

LARGE SCREEN

SOLVE BACK

ASYMETRIC
35% vs 65%
LEFT RIGHT

MOVEABLE

TOO LONG OF A NECK

FIX SEAT

PIVOT

STORAGE

FLAT BOTTOM

93

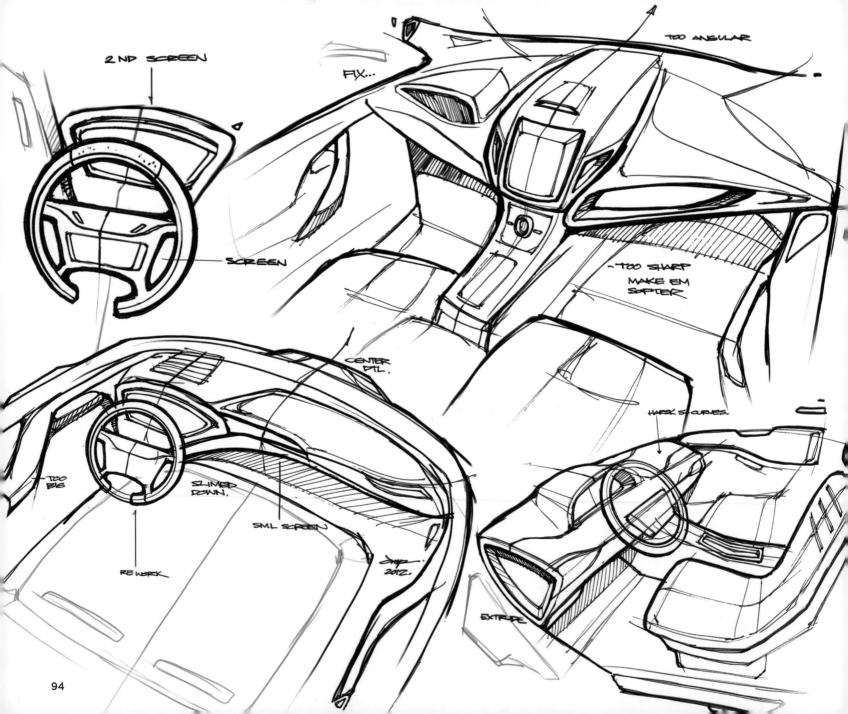

2ND SCREEN

SCREEN

FIX...

TOO ANGULAR

TOO SHARP
MAKE EM
SOFTER

CENTER
DTL.

TOO
BIG

SLIMED
DOWN.

SML SCREEN

REWORK

HARSK S-CURVES.

EXTRUDE

2012.

94

ATX

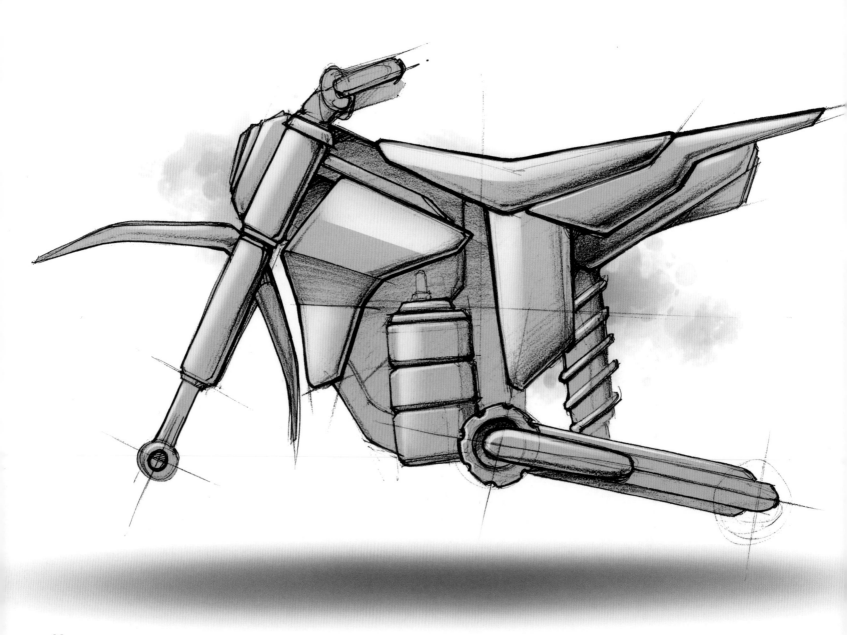

FX

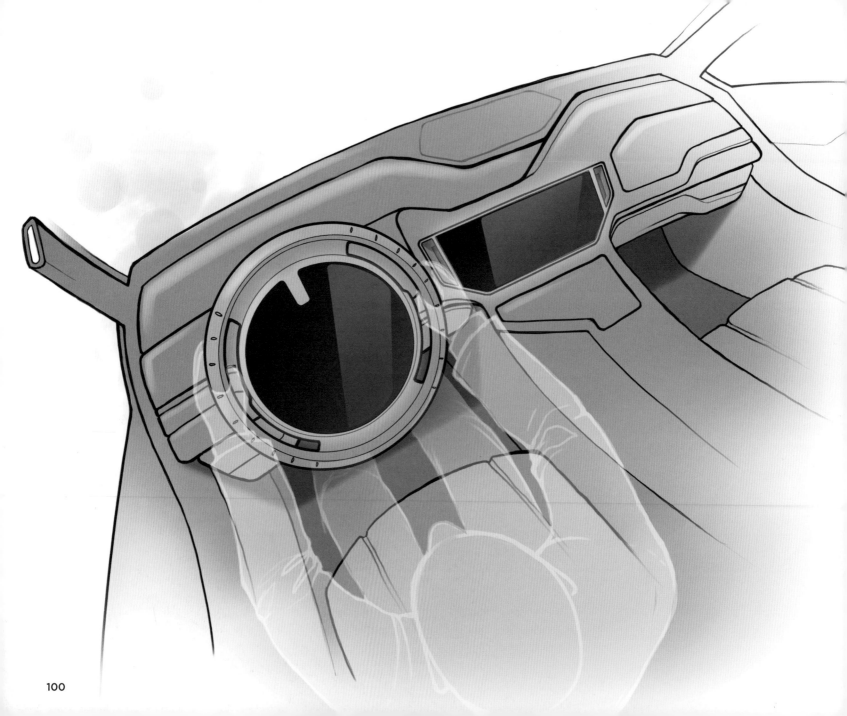

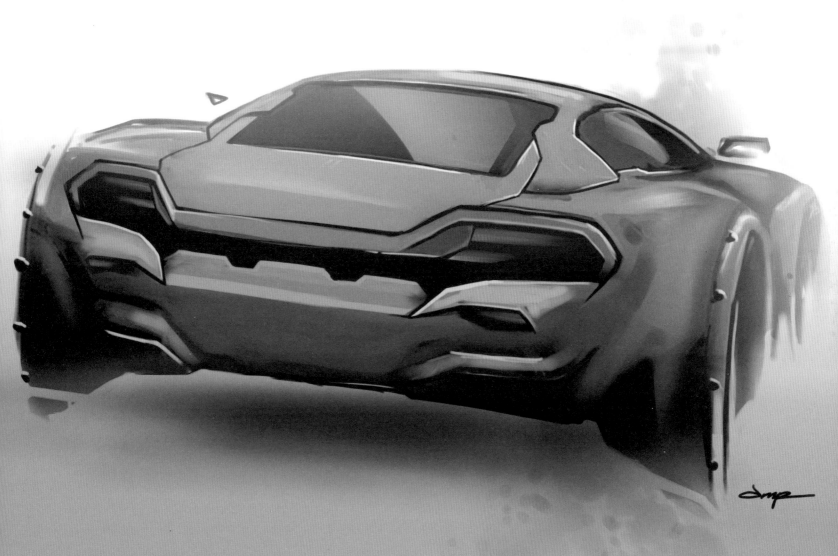

103

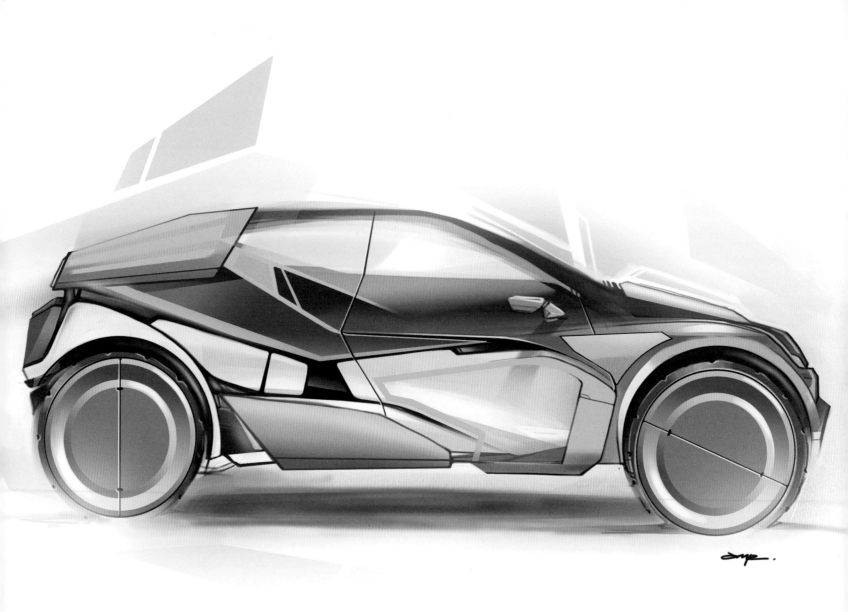

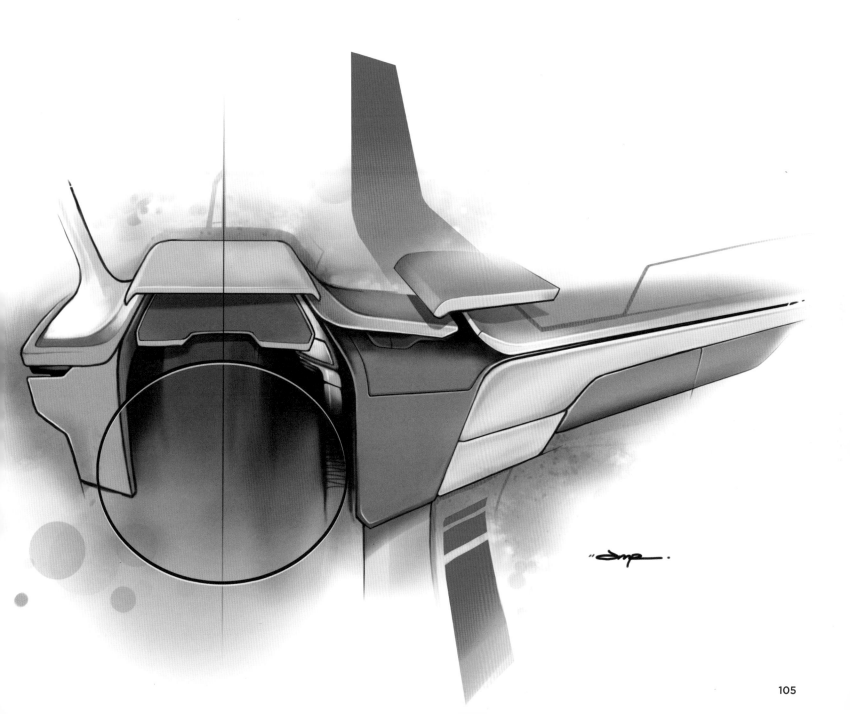

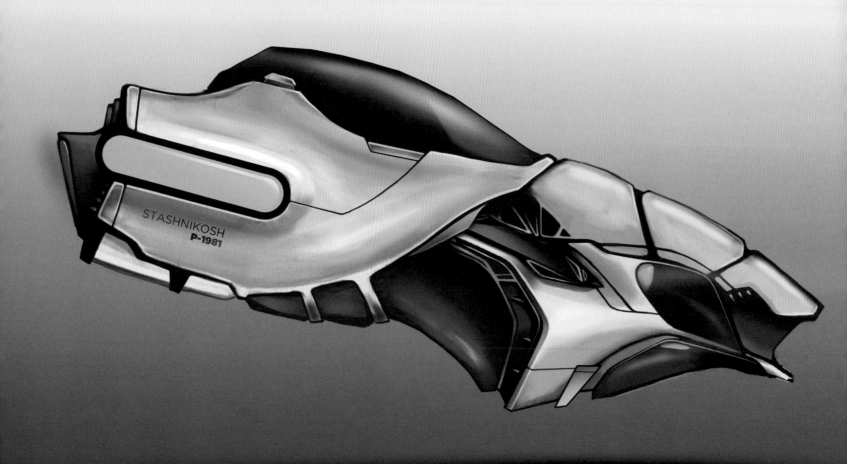

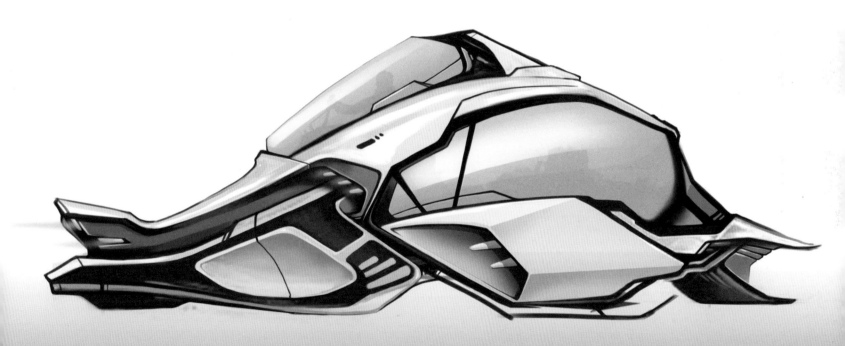

soft
goods

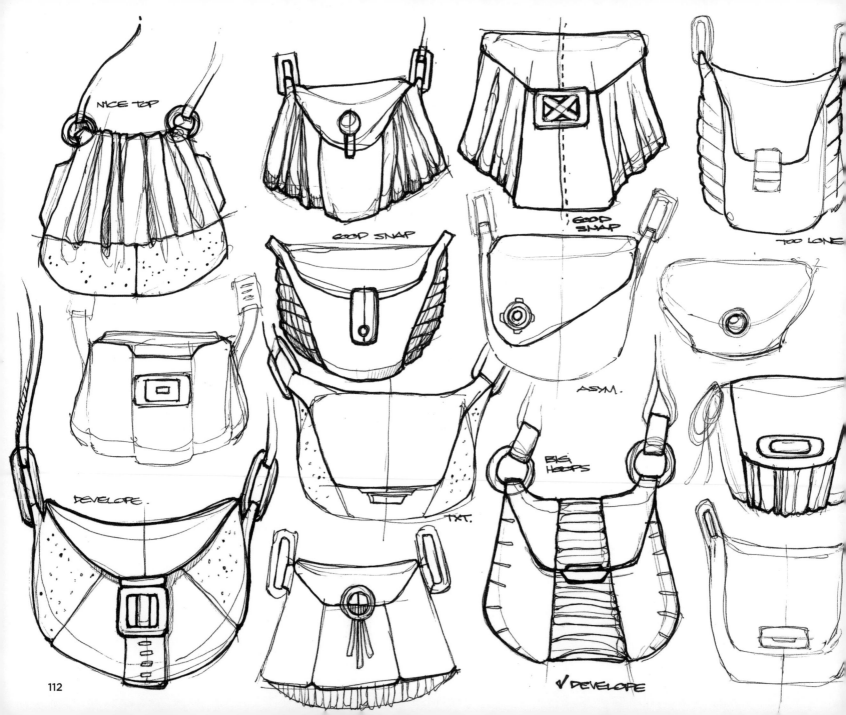

NICE TOP

GOOD SNAP

GOOD SNAP

TOO LONG

DEVELOPE.

TXT.

ASYM.

BIG HOOPS

✓ DEVELOPE

112

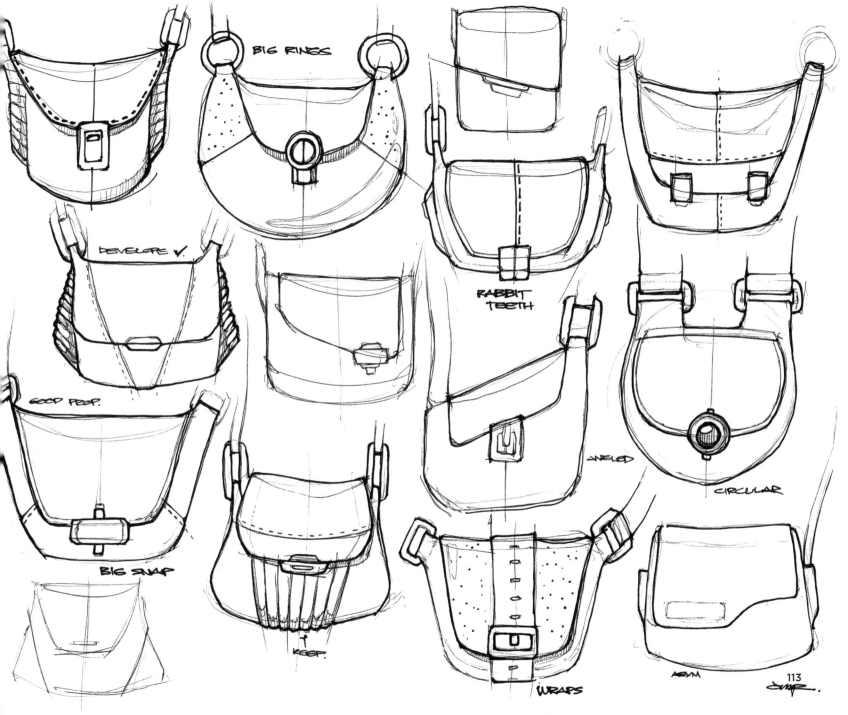

BIG RINGS

DEVELOPE ✓

RABBIT TEETH

GOOD PROP.

BIG SNAP

KEEP

ANGLED

CIRCULAR

WRAPS

ASYM

113

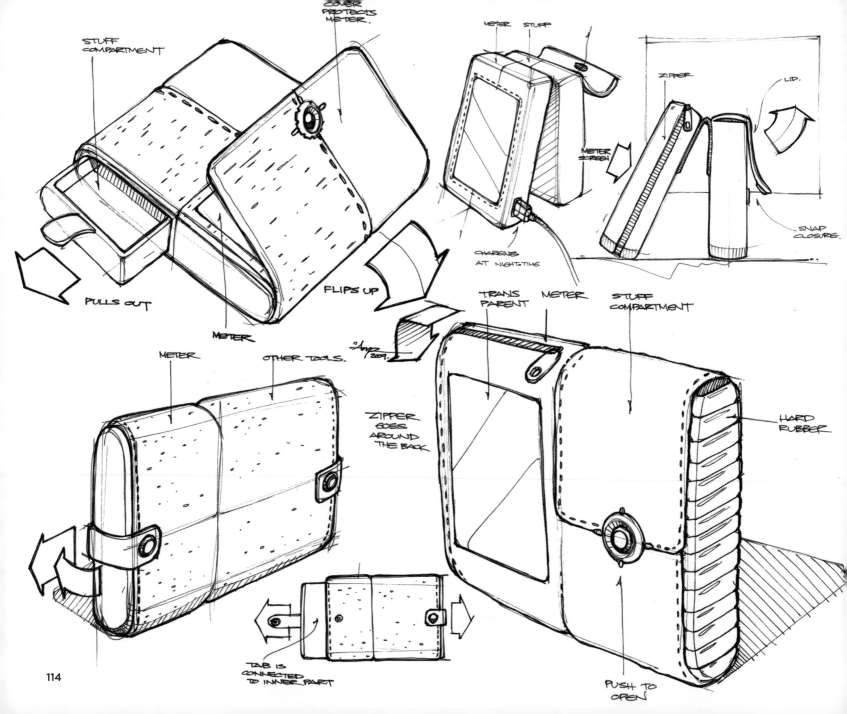

STUFF COMPARTMENT

COVER PROTECTS METER.

PULLS OUT

METER

FLIPS UP

"Amp 2009.

METER STUFF

METER SCREEN

CHARGING AT NIGHT-TIME

ZIPPER

LID.

SNAP CLOSURE.

METER

OTHER TOOLS.

ZIPPER GOES AROUND THE BACK

TRANS PARENT

METER

STUFF COMPARTMENT

HARD RUBBER

PUSH TO OPEN

TAB IS CONNECTED TO INNER PART

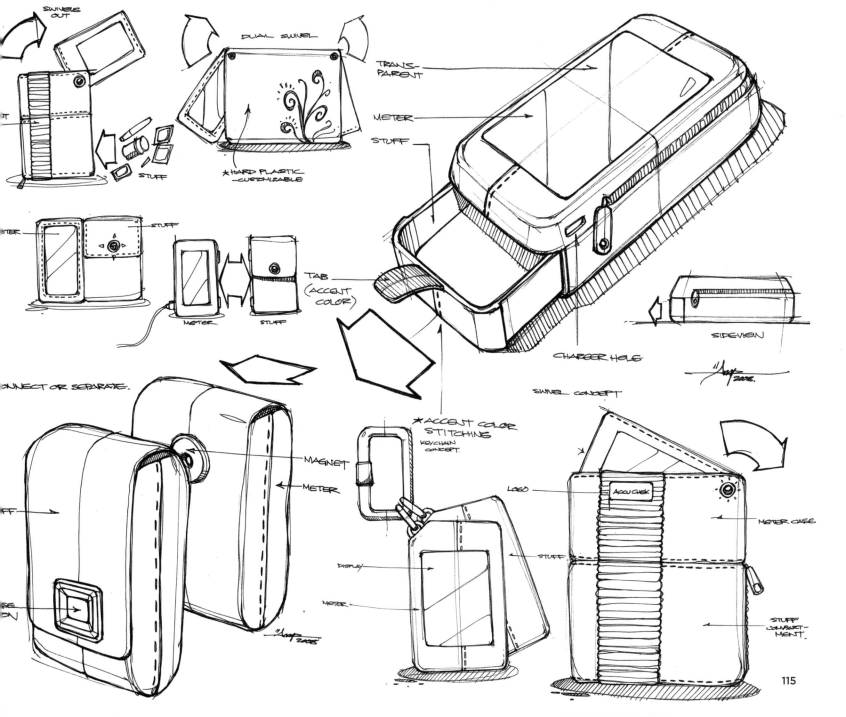

SWIVELS OUT

DUAL SWIVEL

STUFF

★ HARD PLASTIC
CUSTOMIZABLE

TRANS-
PARENT

METER

STUFF

TAB
(ACCENT
COLOR)

CHARGER HOLE

SIDEVIEW

STUFF

METER

STUFF

CONNECT OR SEPARATE.

MAGNET

METER

SWIVEL CONCEPT

★ ACCENT COLOR
STITCHING

KEYCHAIN
CONCEPT.

LOGO

ACCU CHEK

METER CASE

DISPLAY

STUFF

METER

STUFF
COMPART-
MENT.

115

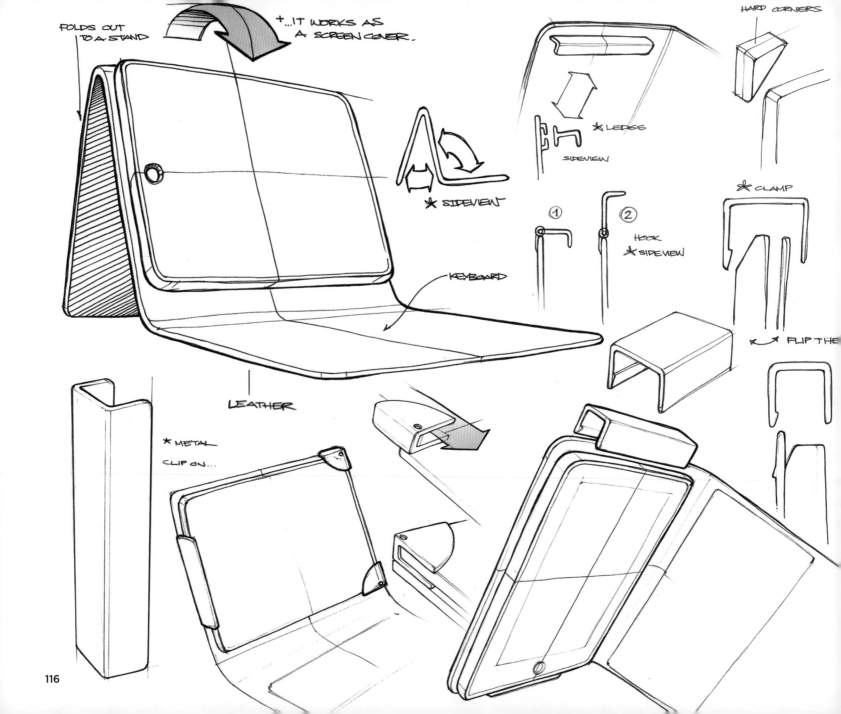

FOLDS OUT TO A STAND

+...IT WORKS AS A SCREEN COVER.

HARD CORNERS

* LEDGE

SIDEVIEW

* SIDEVIEW

① ②

HOOK
* SIDEVIEW

* CLAMP

FLIP THE

KEYBOARD

LEATHER

* METAL
CLIP ON...

116

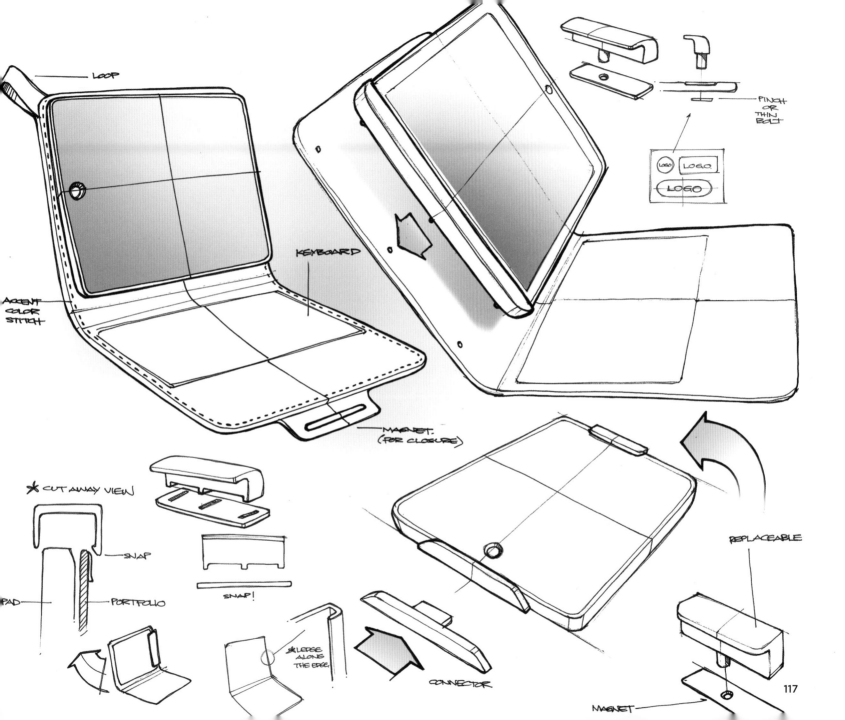

LOOP

ACCENT COLOR STITCH

KEYBOARD

MAGNET (FOR CLOSURE)

PINCH OR THIN BOLT

LOGO   LOGO
LOGO

REPLACEABLE

CONNECTOR

MAGNET

★ CUT AWAY VIEW

SNAP

PAD   PORTFOLIO

SNAP!

★ LEDGE ALONG THE EDGE.

117

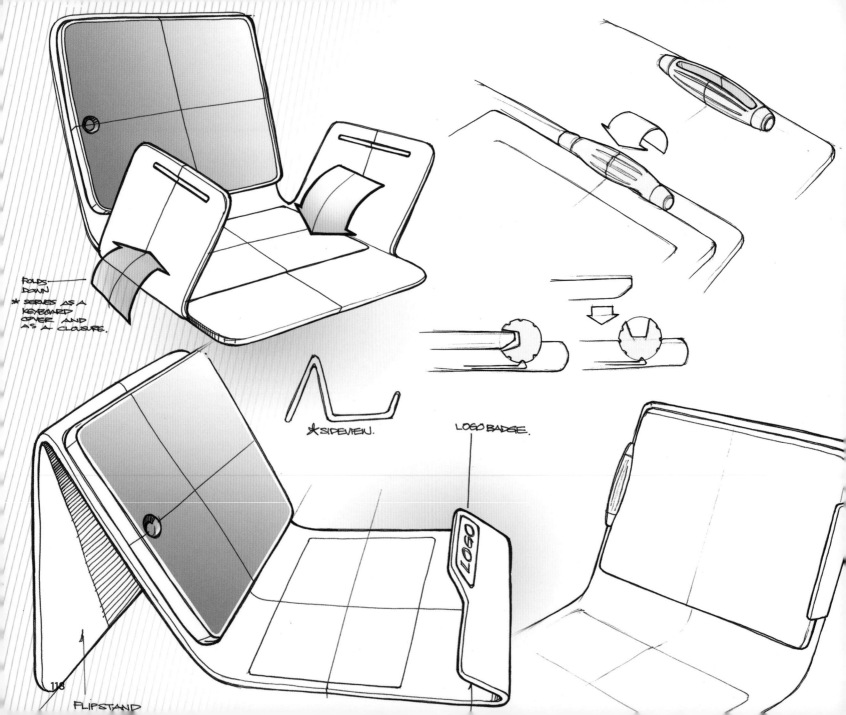

FOLDS.
DOWN

* SERVES AS A
  KEYBOARD
  COVER. AND
  AS A CLOSURE.

*SIDEVIEW.

LOGO BADGE.

LOGO

118

FLIPSTAND

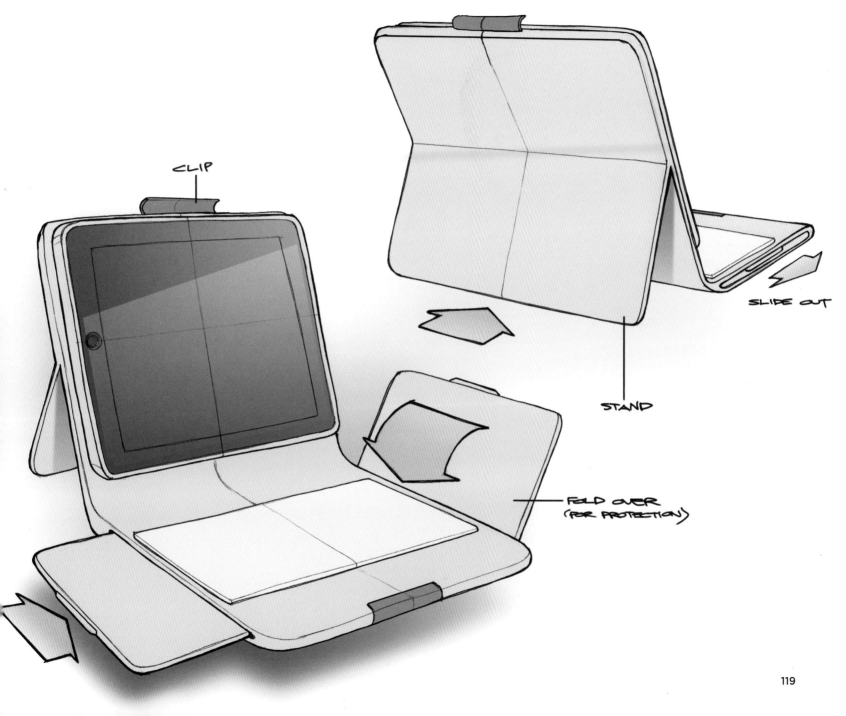

CLIP

STAND

SLIDE OUT

FOLD OVER
(FOR PROTECTION)

119

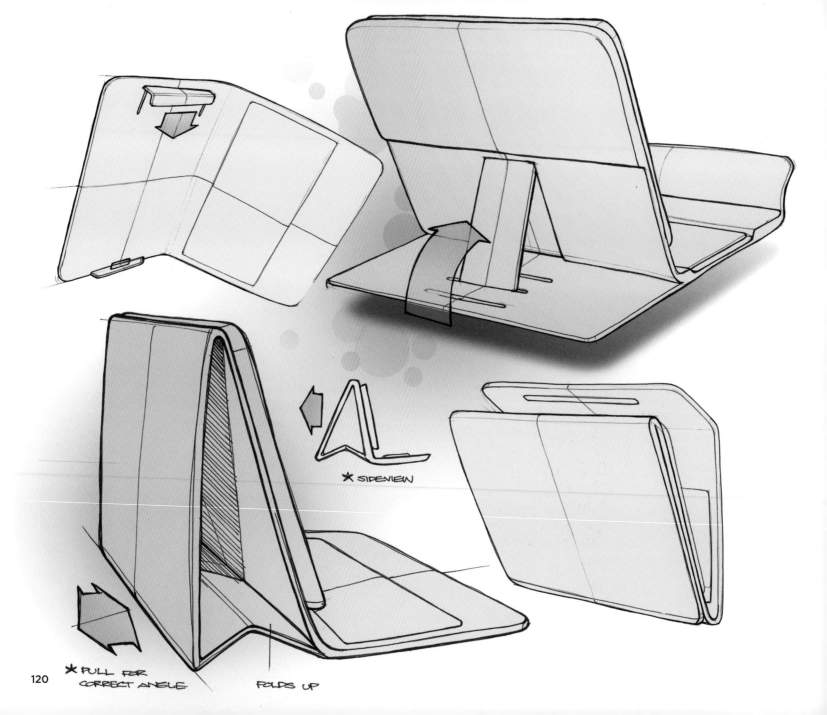

* SIDEVIEW

120

* PULL FOR
CORRECT ANGLE

FOLDS UP

RUBBER EDGE

- KEYBOARD IS FLUSH...

121

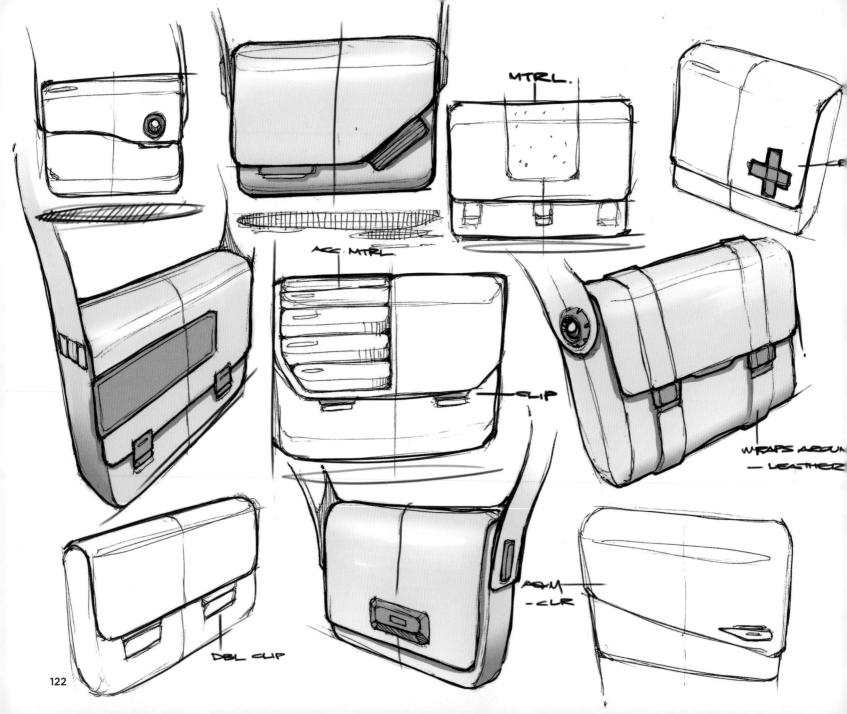

MTRL.

ACC MTRL

CLIP

WRAPS AROUND
— LEATHER

ASM
— CLR

DBL CLIP

122

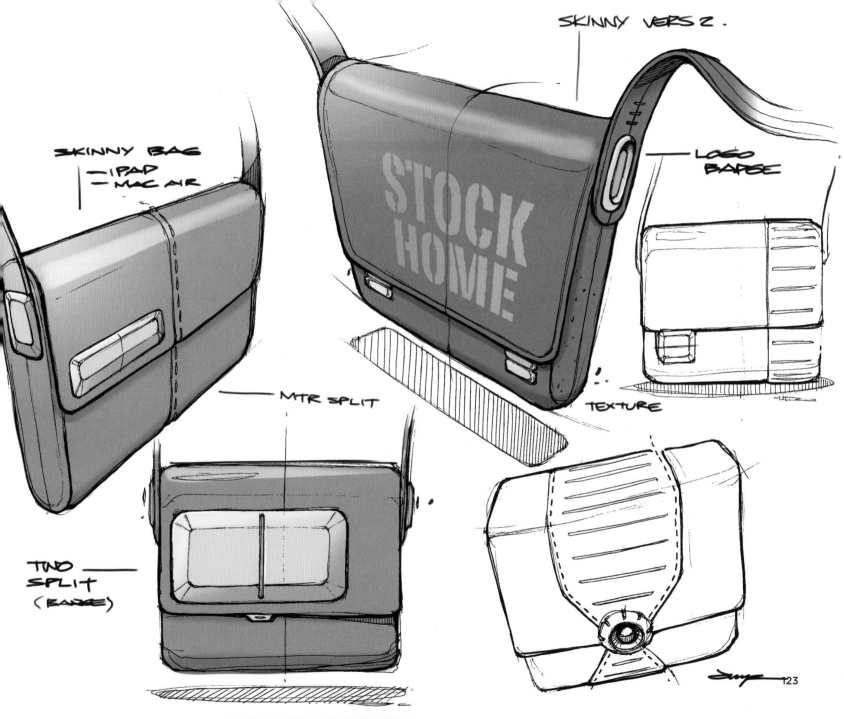

SKINNY VERS 2.

SKINNY BAG
—IPAD
—MAC AIR

LOGO
BADGE

STOCK
HOME

TEXTURE

MTR SPLIT

TWO
SPLIT
(BADGE)

123

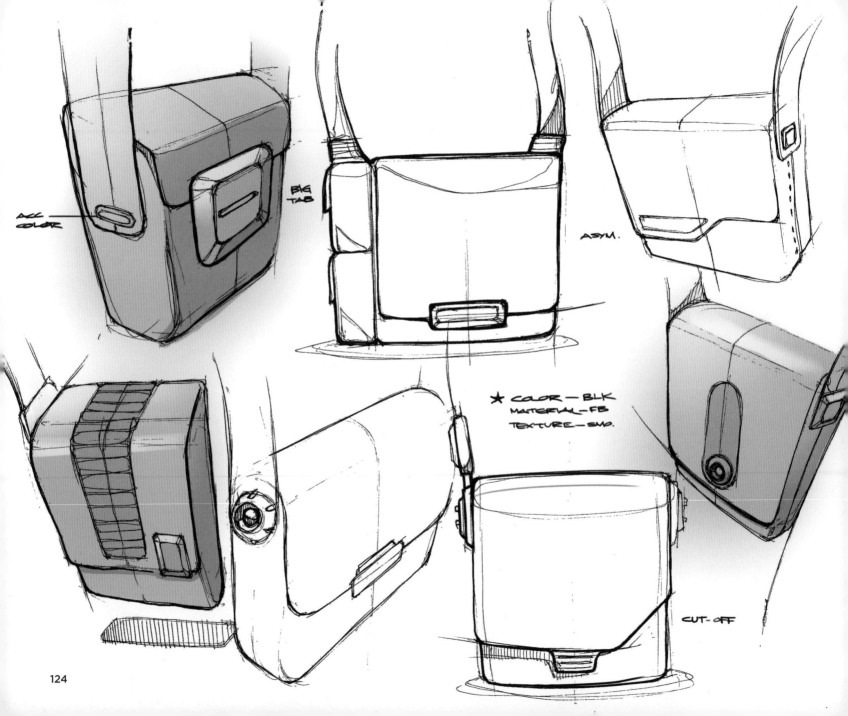

ACC COLOR

BIG TAB

ASYM.

★ COLOR — BLK
MATERIAL — FB
TEXTURE — SMO.

CUT-OFF

124

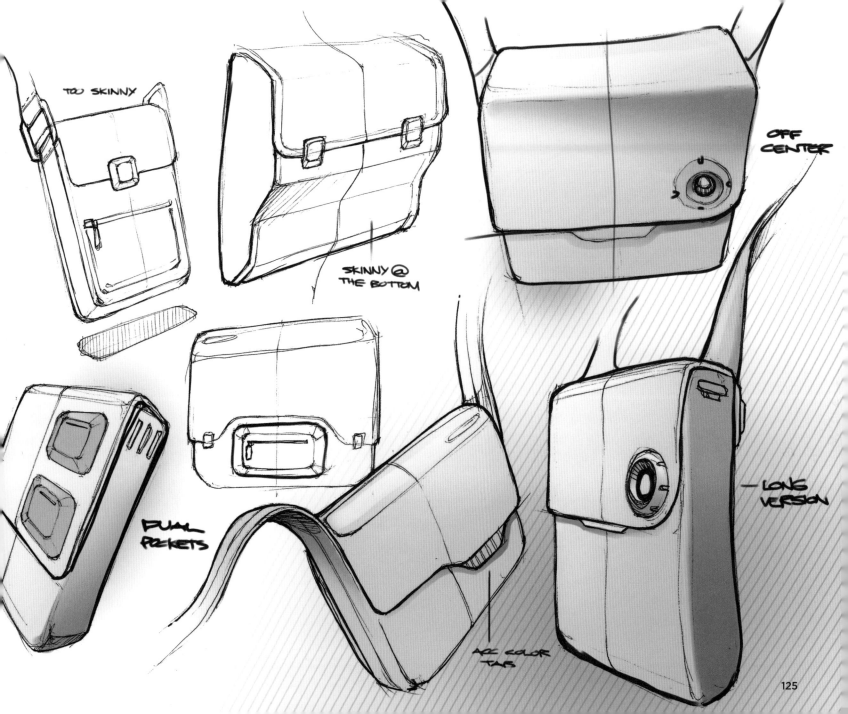

TOO SKINNY

SKINNY @ THE BOTTOM

OFF CENTER

DUAL POCKETS

ARC COLOR TABS

LONG VERSION

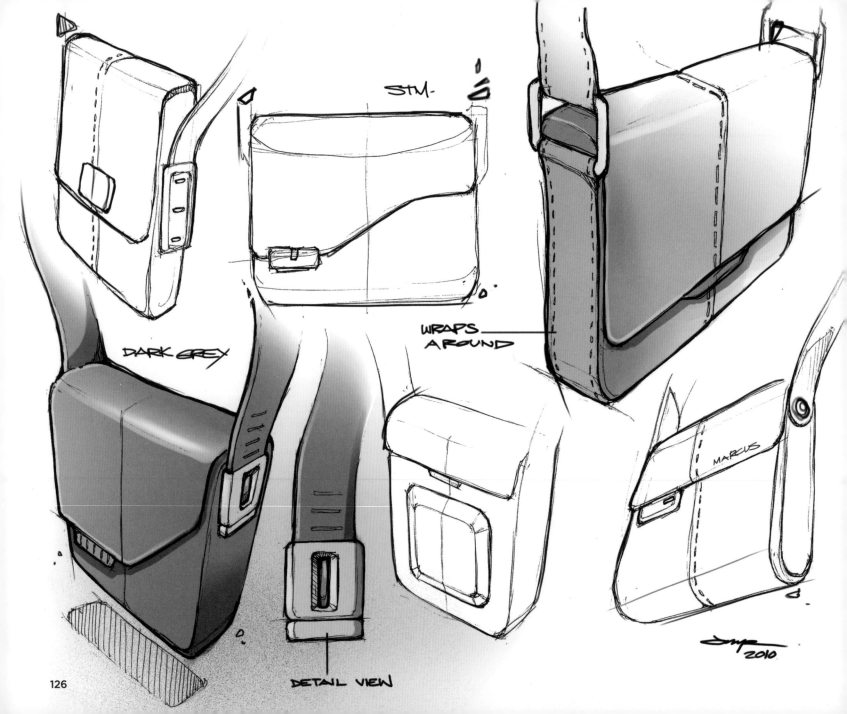

STM-

DARK GREY

WRAPS
AROUND

MARCUS

DETAIL VIEW

2010

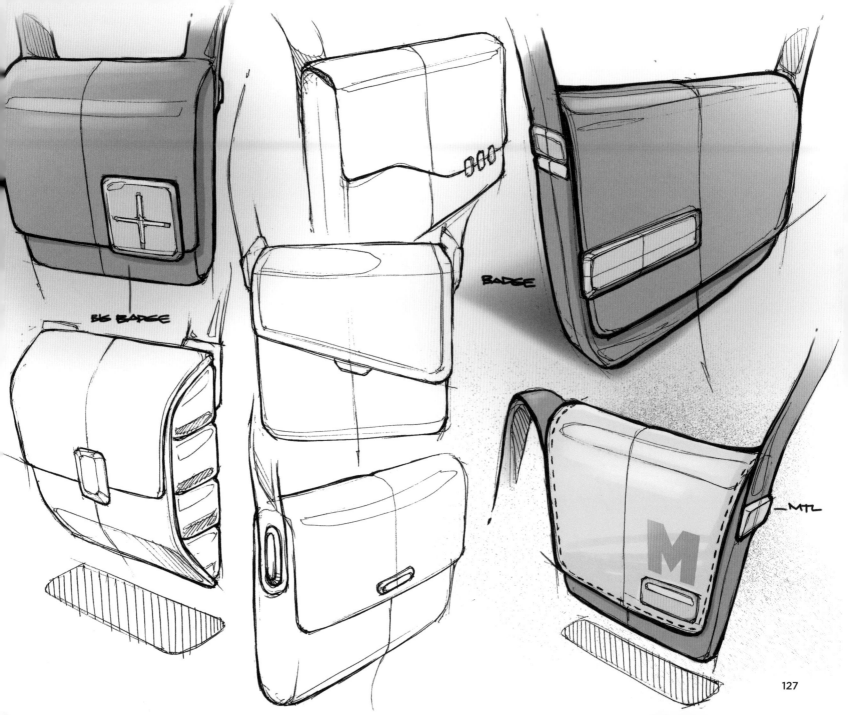

BIG BADGE

BADGE

MTL

M

127

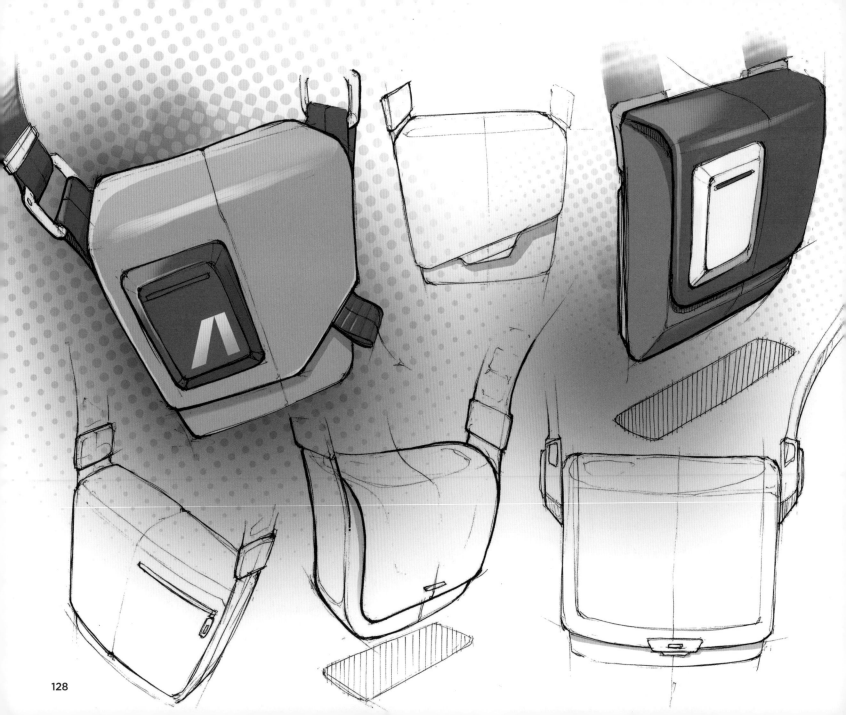

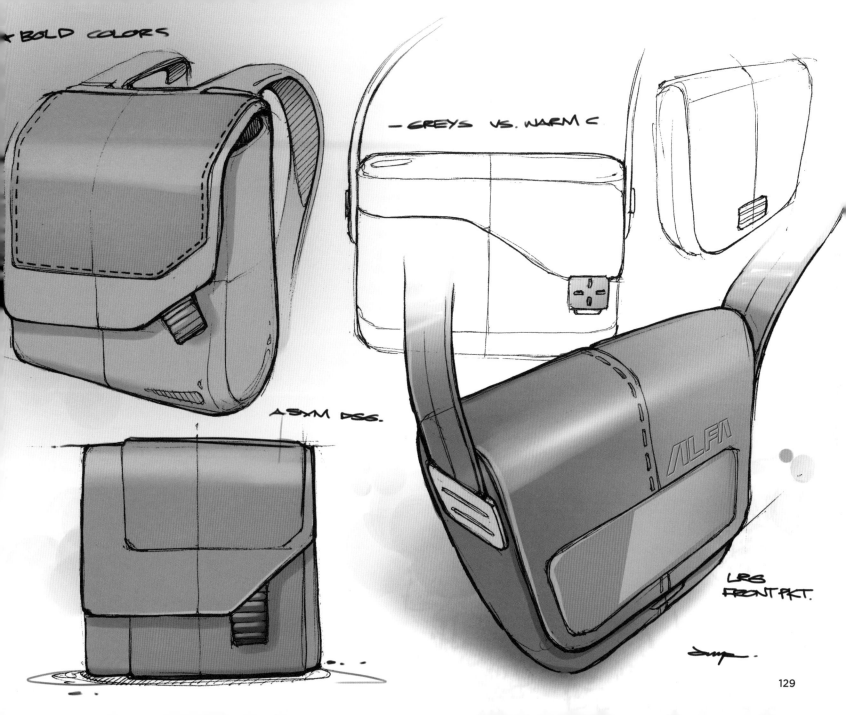

BOLD COLORS

GREYS VS. WARM C

ASYM DSG.

ALFA

LRG
FRONT PKT.

129

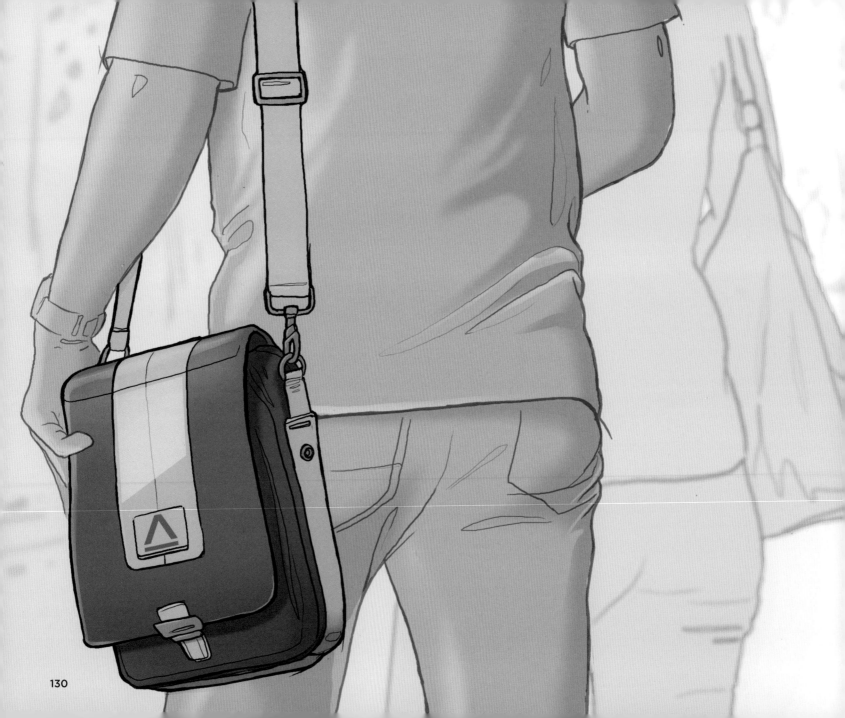

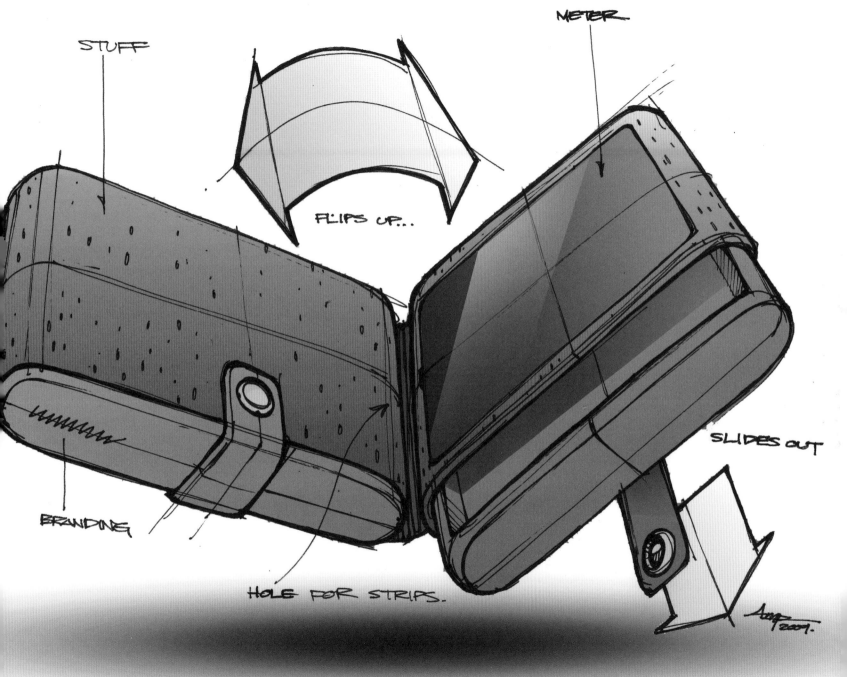

STUFF

METER

FLIPS UP...

BRANDING

HOLE FOR STRIPS.

SLIDES OUT

131

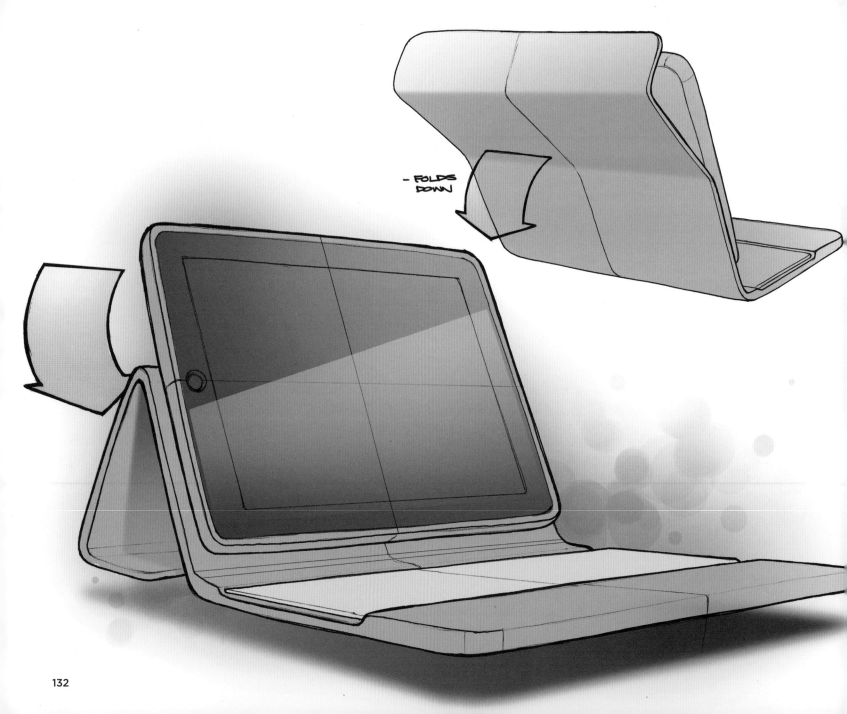

- FOLDS DOWN

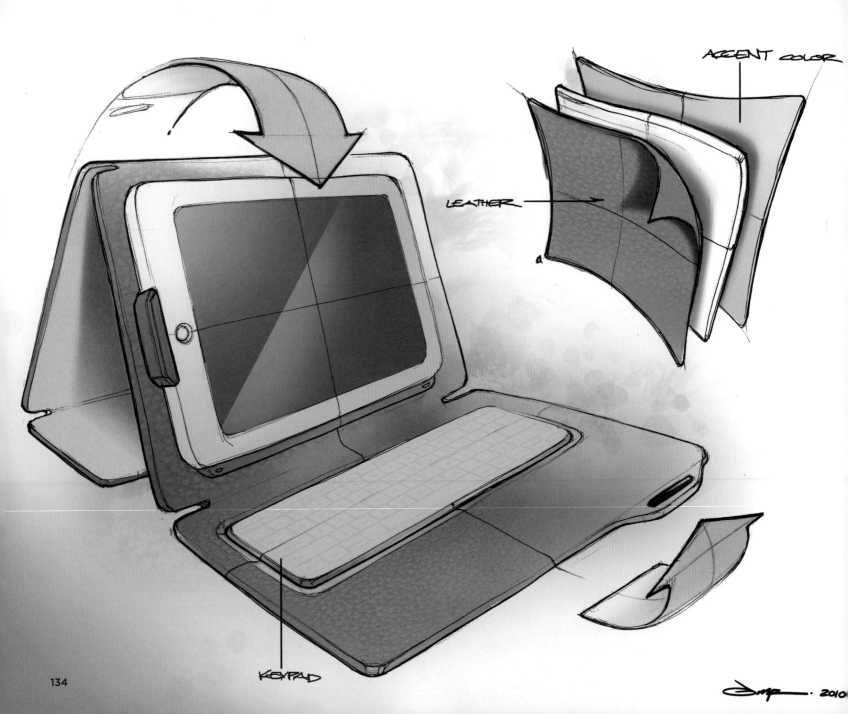

ACCENT COLOR

LEATHER

KEYPAD

2010

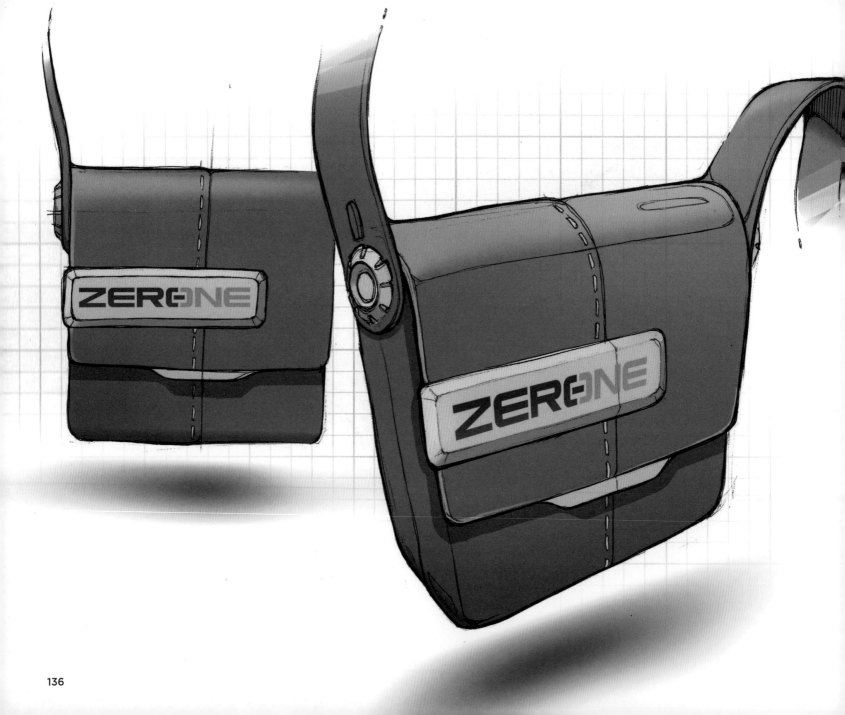

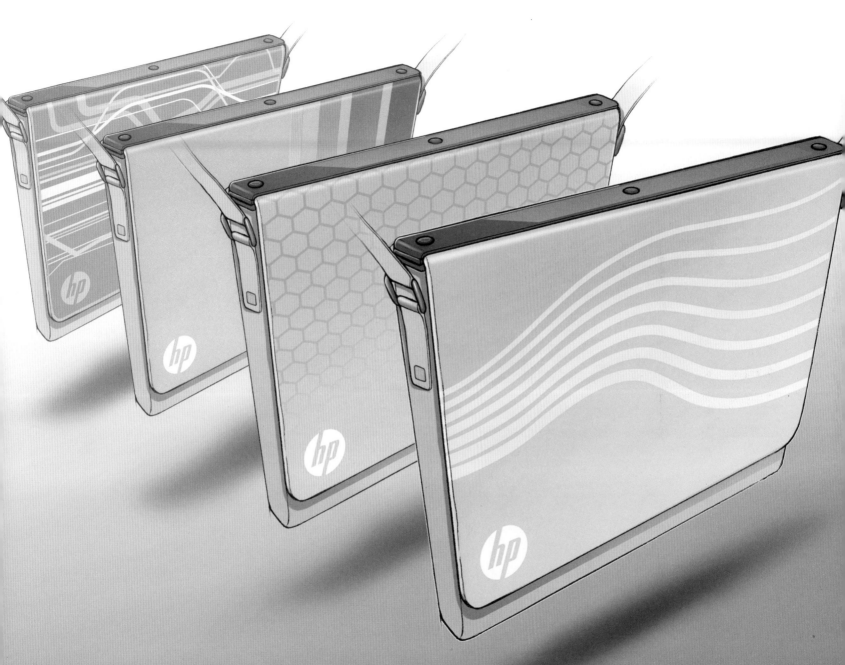

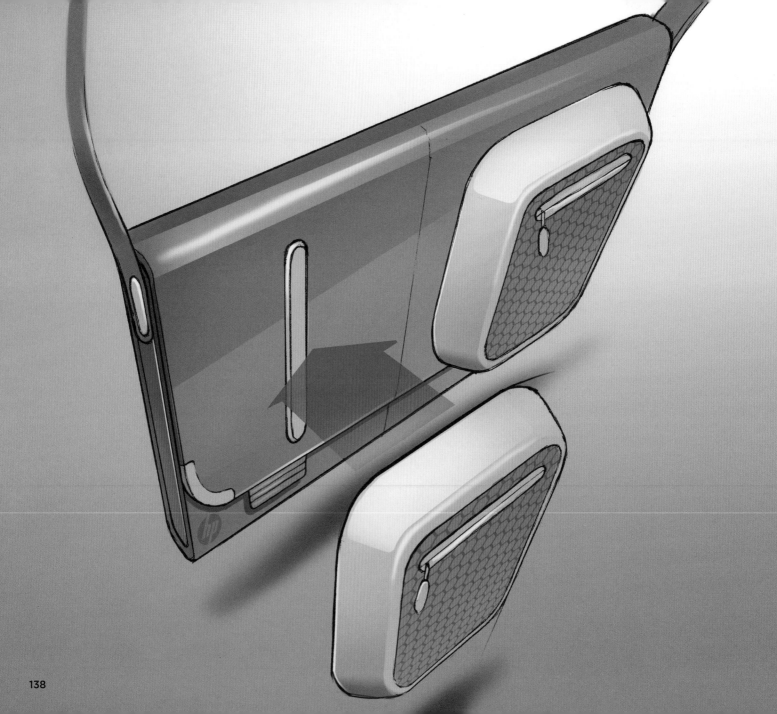

LOWER VS HIGH.

REPE.

LIKE PUMA...

LOW-PROFILE...

COLORS TO
DEAL WITH:
- RED & ORG.

TOP
VIEWS

GOES
LOW

BLACK
MSH.

ALL
BLK

OPEN

STRAP
GOES
THRU

THREE
BREAKS.

D MATERIALS
- BLK
- RED
- MSH.

STICKS OUT.

STRETCHES
BOTH SIDES

DOUBLE
STRAP

NO LACES

ALL
TXTR

HI
GLOSS
DTL.

TOO SPACEY.

THICKER
SOLE

NICE
WRAP

142

SECTION 7

footwear

WRAPS AROUND.

PIVOT.

BACK DETAIL

CENTER IS HIGH GLOSS.

SIDE PANELS ARE STIFF

LOCKED STRAP.

DEVELOPE THIS FURTHER.

DRIPS

LOGO

BLACK + BLUE + ACCENT WHITE.

HARD PLASTIC

PLACE FOR GFX

BACK OVERLAPS

LOOP

PLACE FOR GFX

DEVELOPE THIS FURTHER

FRONT PIECE

BLK

SOLE

* TO BOOT LUGE

BACK MATTE

GRIP.

- I LIKE THESE PROPORTIONS.

TOO LADY GAGAESQUE.

TOO BIG

SPLIT.

SOLE.

BIGGER HOLE

PLACE FOR LOGO

LEATHER

ACC. COLOR

NK

GROW THIS

THIN

FRAGILE

WOOD

WORK WITH THIS...

144

DETAIL IS COOL WORK W/ THIS.

BLACK
VS.
BROWNS.

ORGANIC

NRML

TOO EXTREME?

PUSHED TOO
FAR...

WORK THIS.

CLOSED
TOE

MAKE IT SMALLER.

STRAP

NRML.

TEXTURED

A.C. CLR

145

ACCENT COLOR

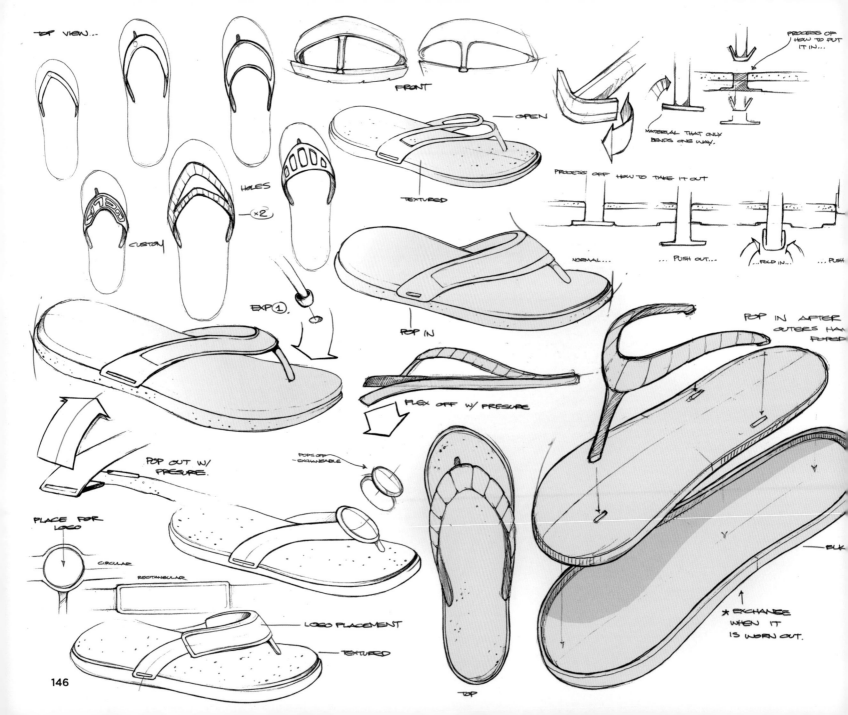

TOP VIEW...

FRONT

OPEN

TEXTURED

HOLES
×2

CUSTOM

EXP 1.

POP IN

PROCESS OF
HOW TO PUT
IT IN...

MATERIAL THAT ONLY
BENDS ONE WAY.

PROCESS OFF HOW TO TAKE IT OUT

NORMAL...   ...PUSH OUT...   ...FOLD IN...   ...PUSH

POP IN AFTER
OUTERS HAVE
FLEXED

FLEX OFF W/ PRESSURE

POP OUT W/
PRESURE.

POPS OFF
- EXCHANGEABLE

PLACE FOR
LOGO

CIRCULAR

RECTANGULAR

LOGO PLACEMENT

TEXTURED

TOP

ELK

★ EXCHANGE
WHEN IT
IS WORN OUT.

146

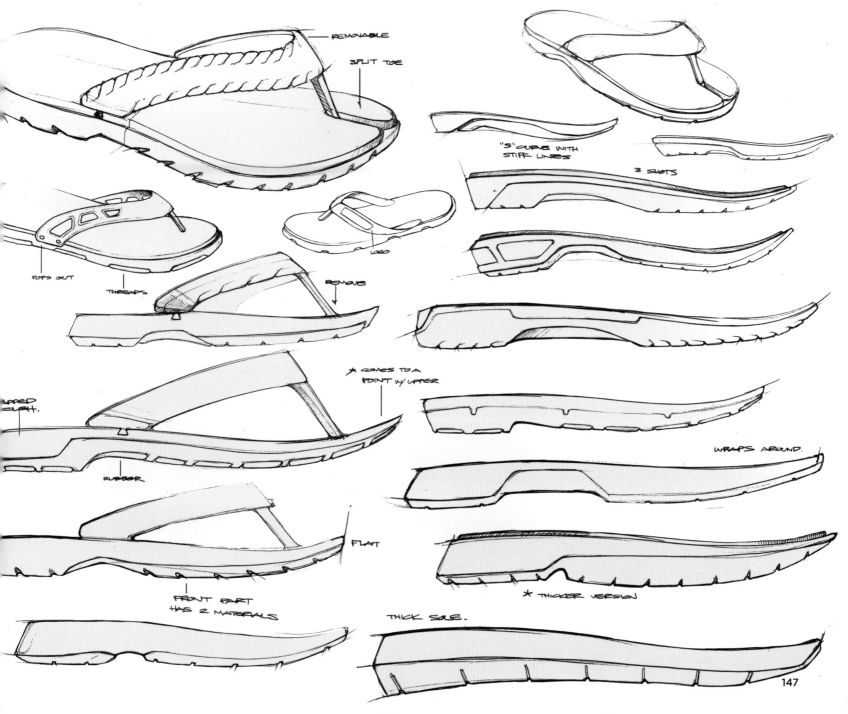

REMOVABLE

SPLIT TOE

"S" CURVE WITH
STIFF LINES

3 SHOTS

POPS OUT

THREADS

LOGO

REMOVE

*COMES TO A
POINT W/ UPPER

WRAPS AROUND.

LAPPED
FLUSH.

RUBBER

FLAT

* THICKER VERSION

FRONT PART
HAS 2 MATERIALS

THICK SOLE.

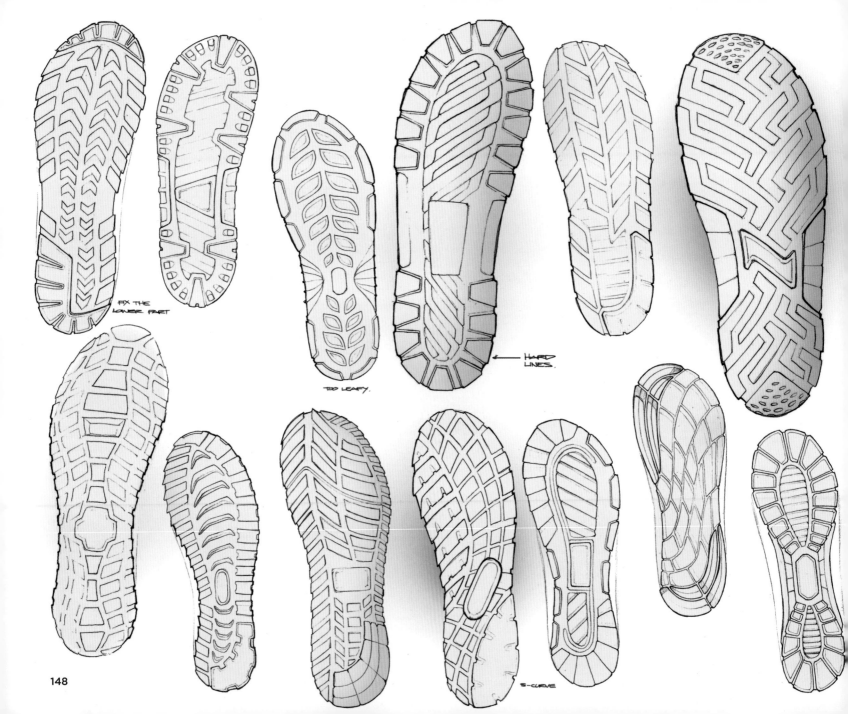

FIX THE
LOWER PART

TOO LEAFY.

← HARD
LINES.

S-CURVE

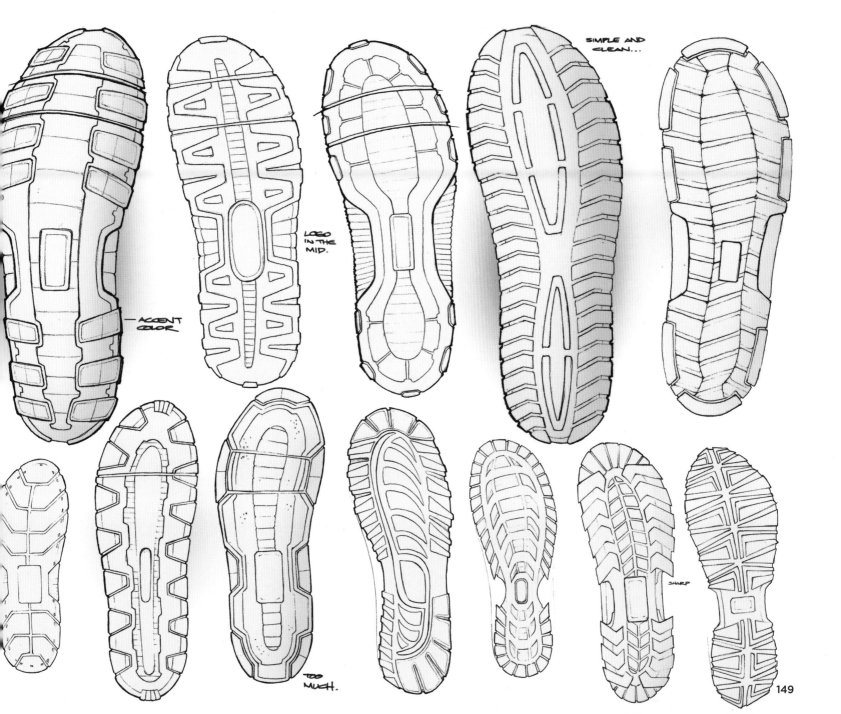

ACCENT COLOR

LOGO IN THE MID.

SIMPLE AND CLEAN...

TOO MUCH.

SHARP

149

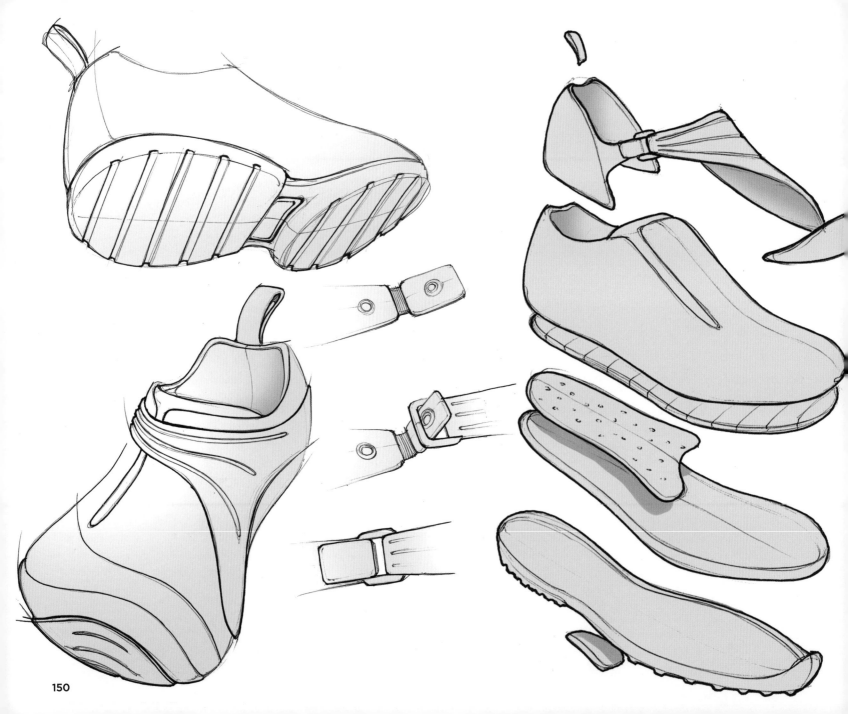

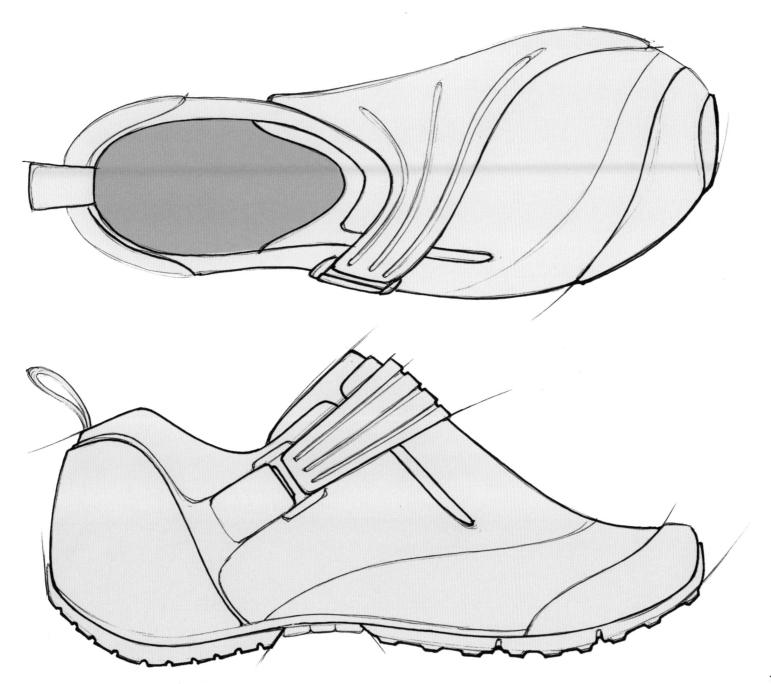

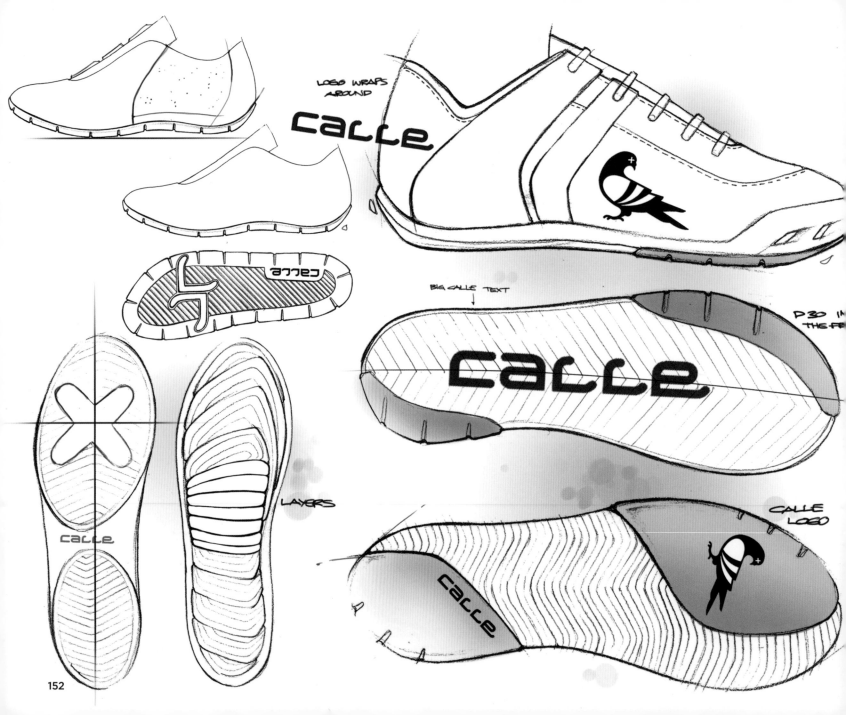

LOGO WRAPS AROUND

CALLE

BIG CALLE TEXT

CALLE

P30 IN
THE FR...

CALLE
LOGO

LAYERS

CALLE

CALLE

152

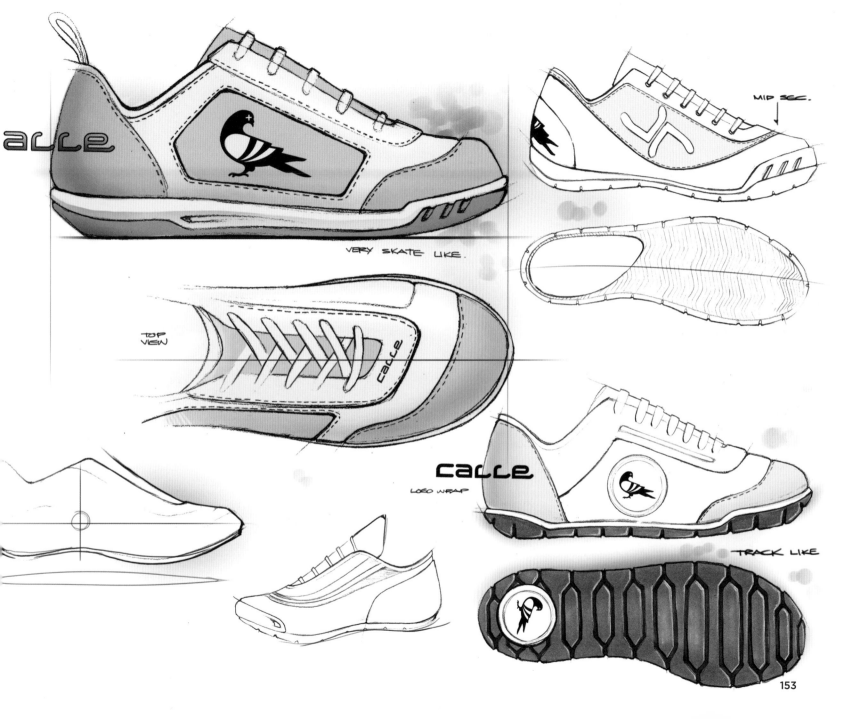

CALLE

VERY SKATE LIKE.

MID SEC.

TOP
VIEW

CALLE

LOGO WRAP

TRACK LIKE

CALLE

153

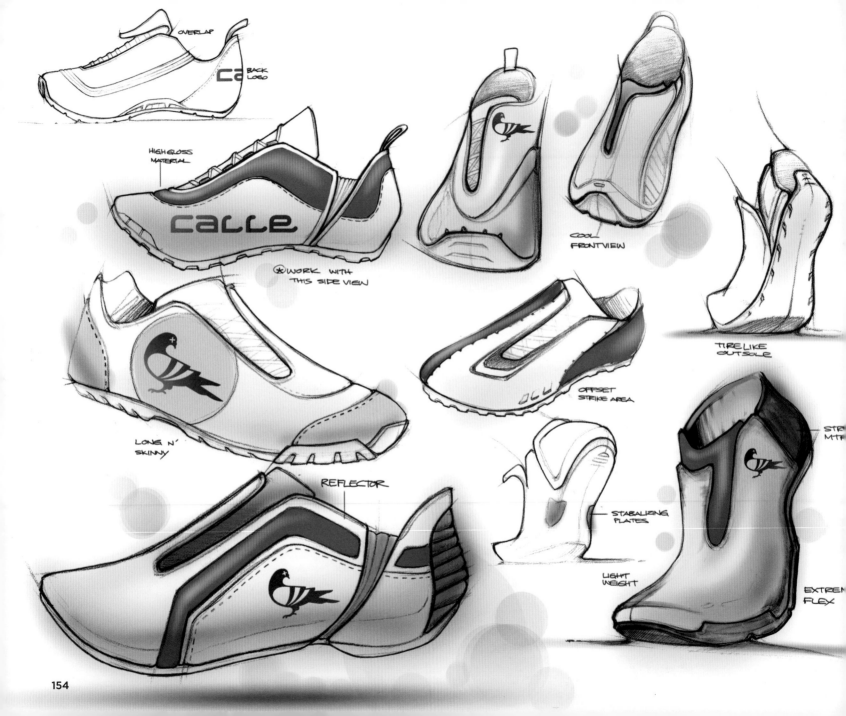

OVERLAP

BACK LOGO

HIGH GLOSS MATERIAL

CALLE

★WORK WITH THIS SIDE VIEW

COOL FRONTVIEW

TIRE LIKE OUTSOLE

LONG N' SKINNY

OFFSET STRIKE AREA

REFLECTOR

STABALIZING PLATES

STR MTR

LIGHT WEIGHT

EXTREM FLEX

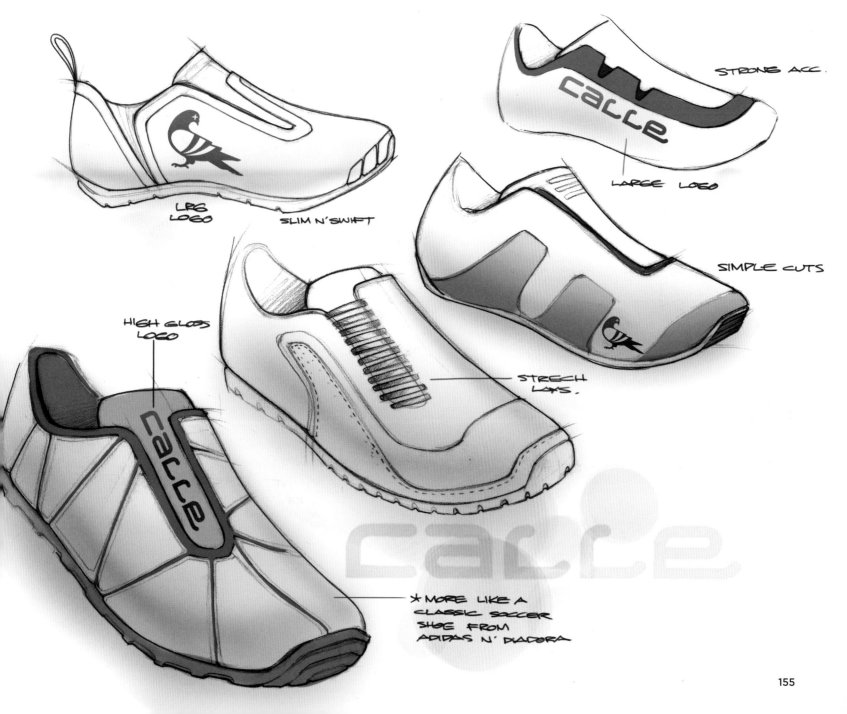

LRG
LOGO

SLIM N'SWIFT

STRONG ACC.

LARGE LOGO

SIMPLE CUTS

HIGH GLOSS
LOGO

STRECH
LXS.

* MORE LIKE A
CLASSIC SOCCER
SHOE FROM
ADIDAS N' DIADORA

155

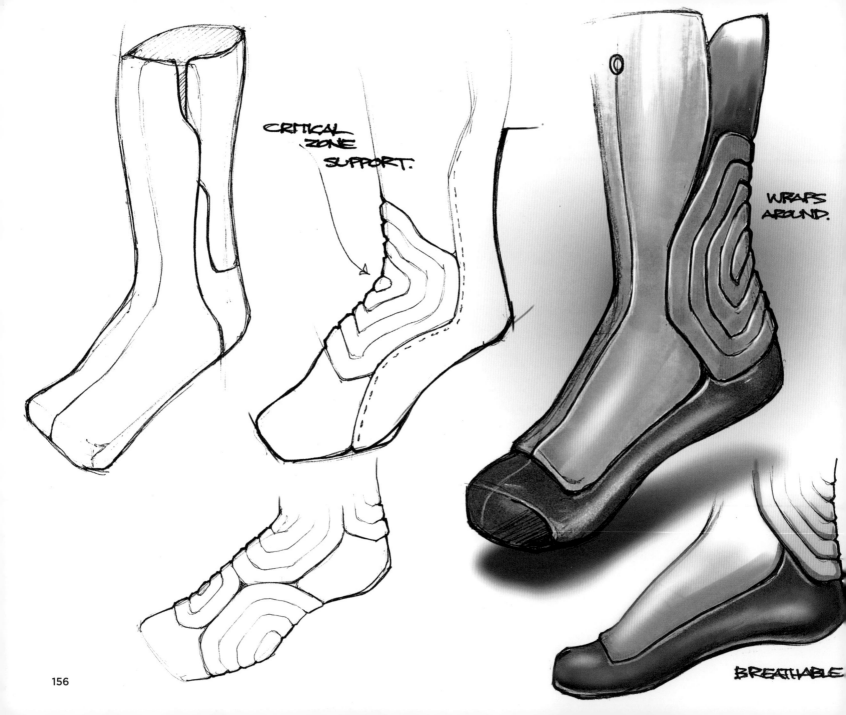

CRITICAL ZONE SUPPORT.

WRAPS AROUND.

BREATHABLE

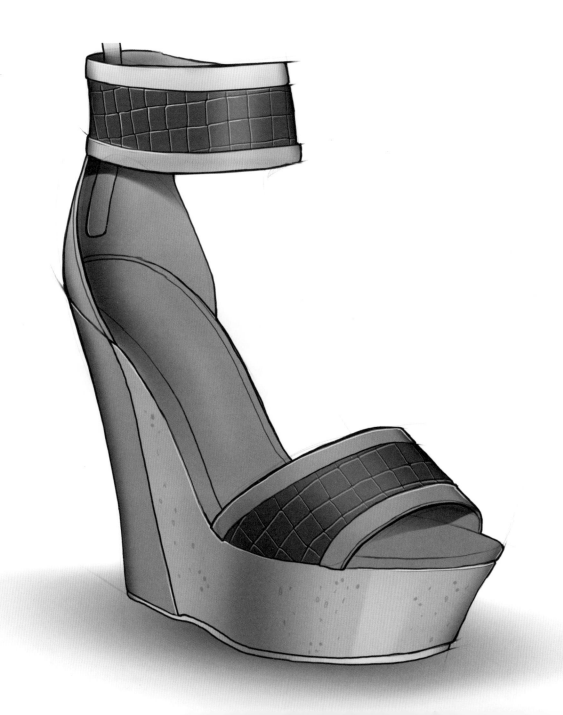

GAZ

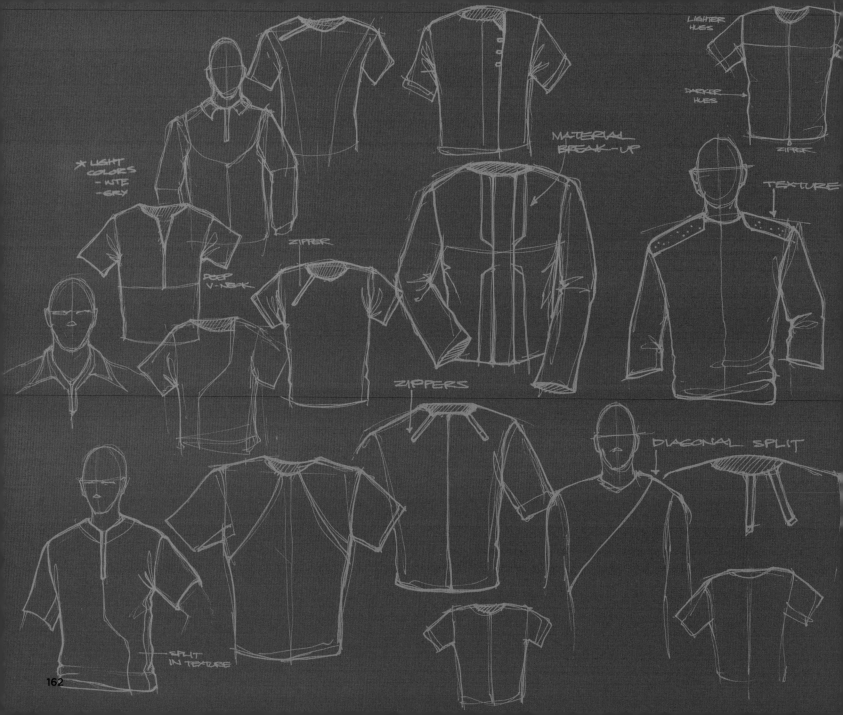

* LIGHT
COLORS
- WTE
- GRY

ZIPPER

DEEP
V-NECK

MATERIAL
BREAK-UP

ZIPPERS

LIGHTER
HUES

DARKER
HUES

ZIPPER

TEXTURE

DIAGONAL SPLIT

SPLIT
IN TEXTURE

162

SECTION 8

apparel

STRIPES ON THE LOWER PART

* COLOR AND MATERIAL BREAKUP

DIAGONAL STYLE
*COLOR

FOLD

LIGHT COLOR

DARK DENIM

*TOO FLOWER-LIKE WORK IN IT...

SHORT @ WAIST

BLK

– TIGHT

HIGH CONTRAST

FLOW

SYMETRIC –
SPLIT
IN LAYERS

DRAWING
FOCUS TO
THE SHOULDERS

POINT

DIAGONAL
CUTS...

LAYERS
– DIF. COLORS

LOTS OF
FLOW

POINT

164

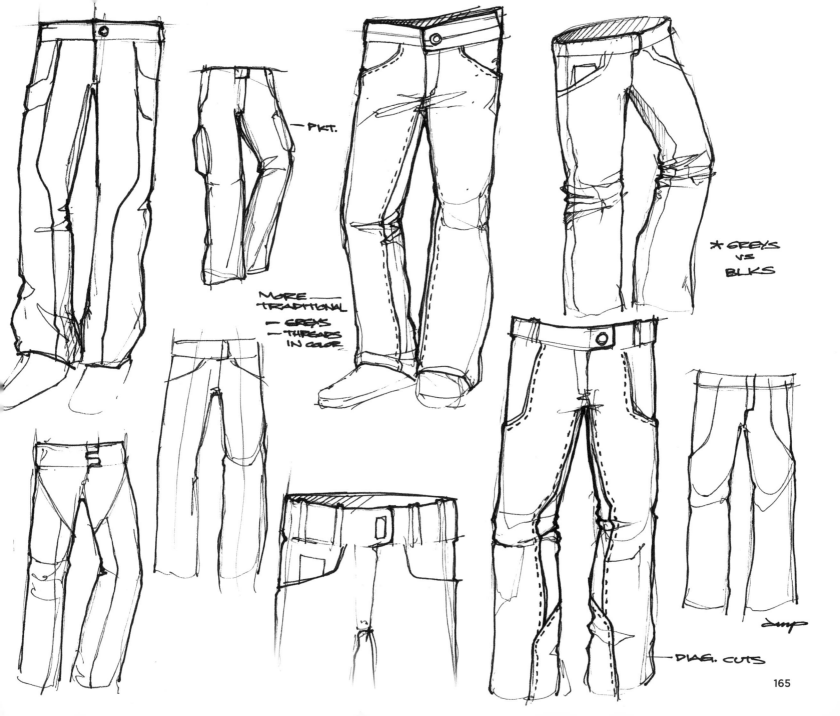

PKT.

MORE
TRADITIONAL
— GREYS
— THREADS
IN COLOR

* GREYS
VS
BLKS

DIAG. CUTS

165

ZIPPER

BLK

MATERIAL CHANGE

DIF. MATERIAL

DEEP NECK

ACCENT

BIT LONGER SLEAVE.

CRIS CROSS

SPLIT

LOGO

SML TURTLE NECK

GAZ

TOO HEAVY DTL

SHORT

166

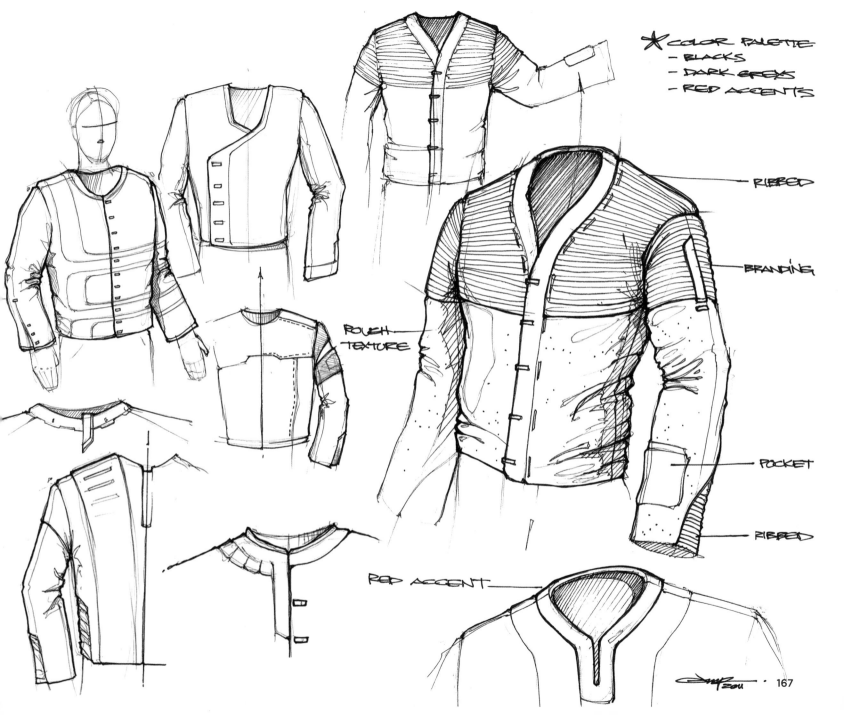

★ COLOR PALETTE
- BLACKS
- DARK GREYS
- RED ACCENTS

RIBBED

BRANDING

ROUGH TEXTURE

POCKET

RIBBED

RED ACCENT

167

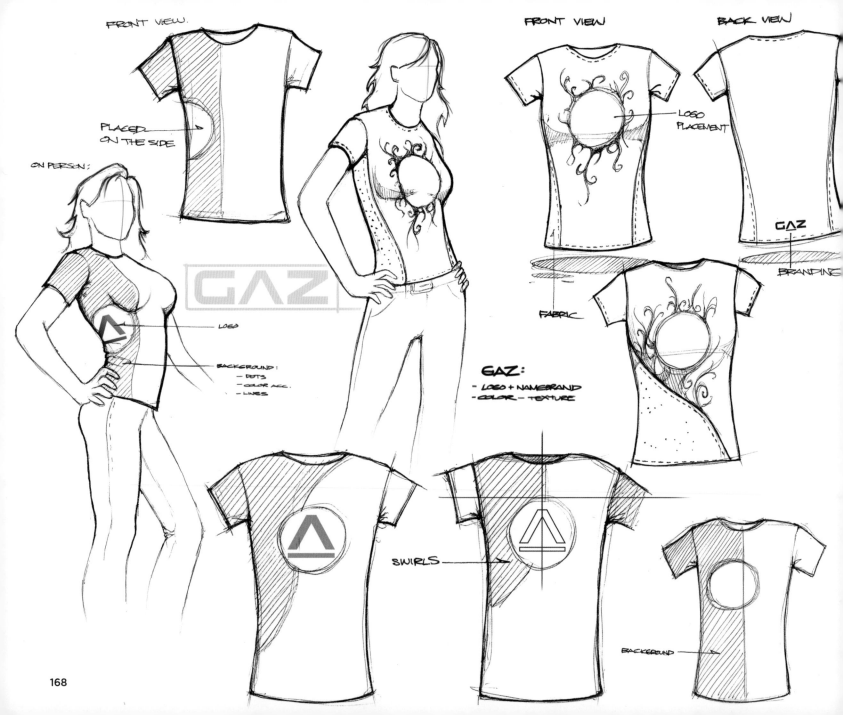

FRONT VIEW.

PLACED
ON THE SIDE

ON PERSON:

GAZ

LOGO

BACKGROUND:
- DOTS
- COLOR ACC.
- LINES

FRONT VIEW

BACK VIEW

LOGO
PLACEMENT

GAZ

BRANDING

FABRIC

GAZ:
- LOGO + NAMEBRAND
- COLOR - TEXTURE

SWIRLS

BACKGROUND

168

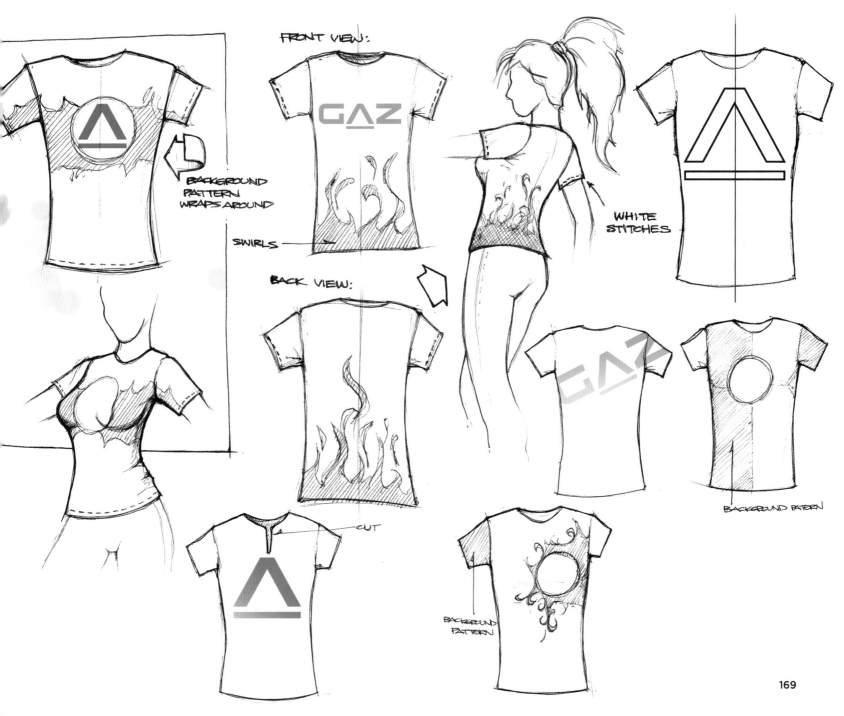

BACKGROUND PATTERN WRAPS AROUND

FRONT VIEW:

GAZ

SWIRLS

BACK VIEW:

CUT

WHITE STITCHES

BACKGROUND PATTERN

BACKGROUND PATTERN

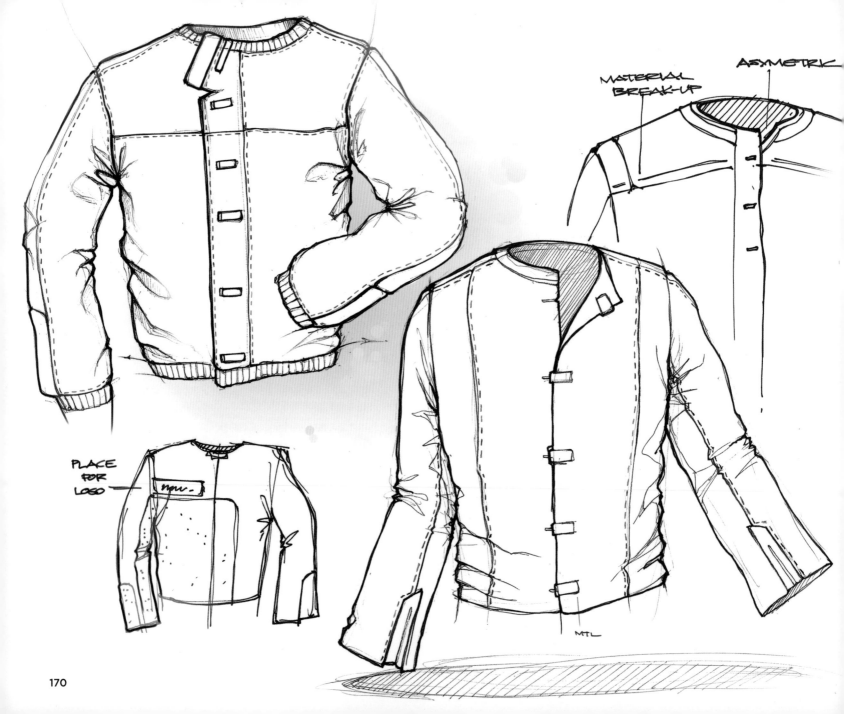

MATERIAL BREAK-UP

ASYMETRIK

PLACE FOR LOGO

now

MTL

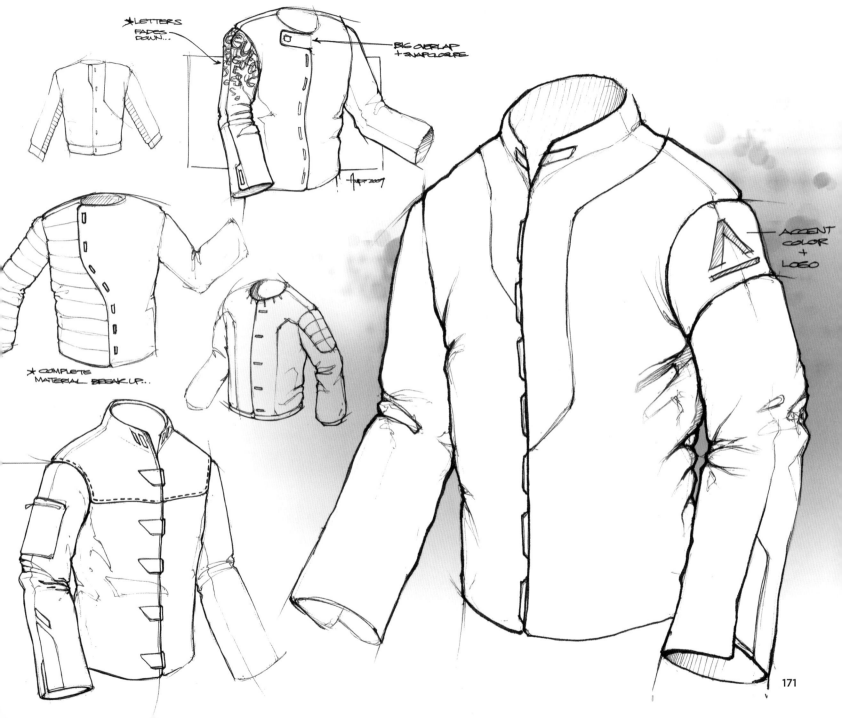

*LETTERS FADES DOWN...

BIG OVERLAP + SNAP CLOSURE

* COMPLETE MATERIAL BREAK UP...

ACCENT COLOR + LOGO

171

ACCENT

DIF. MATERIAL

SEMI DUR.

SHOULDER
SHOULD BE
THE ACCENT
COLOR:
= ORG.
= GRE.
= BLU.

XTRA
PADDING

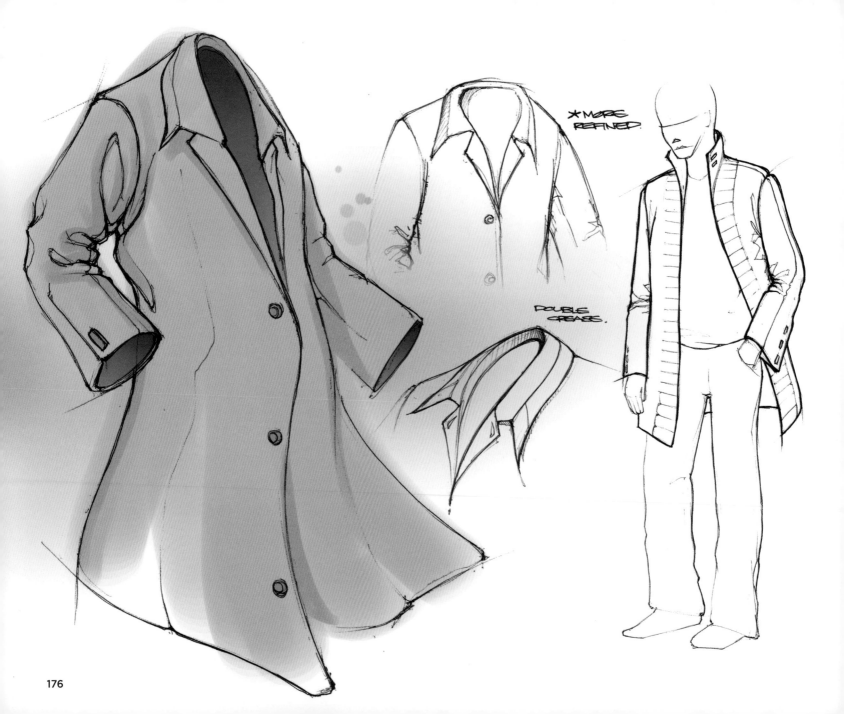

*MORE REFINED.

DOUBLE CREASE.

* SNOWBOARD
CONCEPT
— SHORT
— LIGHT

GAZ

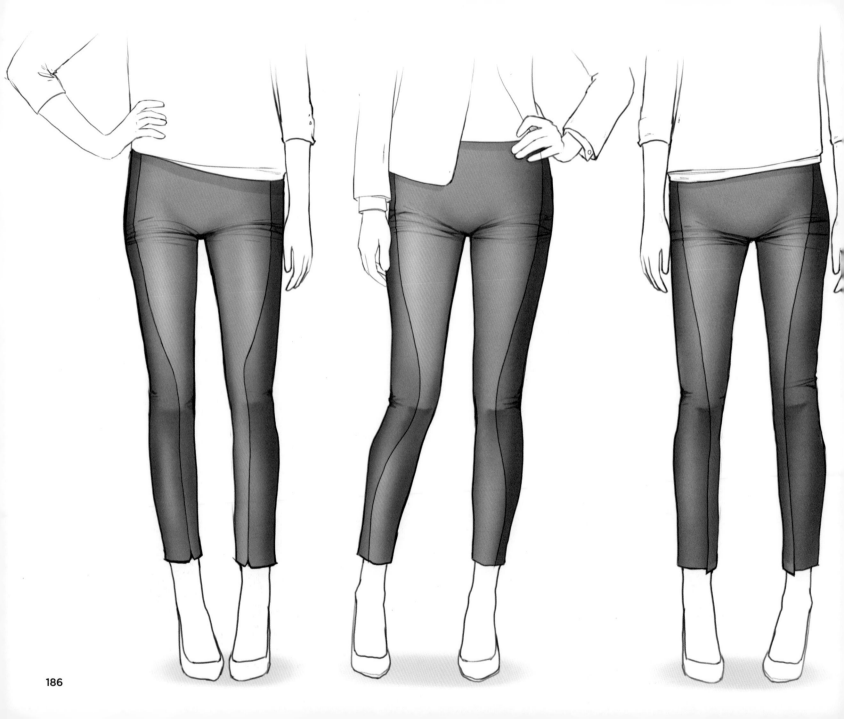

I was born and raised in Stockholm, Sweden, but my family roots are in Santiago, Chile. One of the great blessings I had as a youngster was having the opportunity to travel to many of the beautiful areas of Europe. Seeing cities like Barcelona, Venice, Athens and Copenhagen left a big impression on me. The people, the buildings, the landscapes and colors, all became a part of my visual library. I am grateful today for the sacrifice that my parents made in putting aside money so that we could have these experiences.

For as long as I can remember, drawing has always been one of my favorite activities. For me, drawing is like therapy, and probably one of the few constants that I have had in my life. It gives me joy and a sense of accomplishment.

I remember as a five year old seeing a painting representing a skull and some text I couldn't read, on a wall along the blue line in the Stockholm subway. I was mesmerized by it... I had never seen something like it before. My older brother explained to me that it was a graffiti painting made with spray paint. I spent many train rides after that with my face glued to the window so I could catch a glimpse of that graffiti painting for just a few seconds as we sped by. In my early teens, I was once again captured by the visual language of graffiti. This time around it wasn't enough to me to be a mere spectator and I began to spend countless hours on illustrations, painting murals and doing graphic prints for a variety of corporations, schools and magazines in Sweden, Denmark, Spain, and Italy. The boldness of colors and shapes of graffiti art are still prevalent in my design work today.

I discovered industrial design in 2004 and began my education the same year at Brigham Young University. I was fortunate to be surrounded by bright, hard-working, and extremely talented fellow design students and teachers that pushed me to strive for excellence.

I have been working as a design consultant since 2007. During these years I have had the opportunity to work for such companies as: Microsoft, Samsung, Pepsico, LG, BlackBerry, Good Year, McDonalds and SCJ.

I would like to thank a few individuals that have helped me in this endeavor:

Rudolf van Wezel and BIS publishers for reaching out to me and making this possible.

MaryAnn Parada for her constant support in my completing this project. Marcus Parada and Antonio Parada for the flow of inspiration and joy they always bring me. My parents Lucy and Julio for life itself and for helping me discover the world at a young age. Pablo Parada for believing in me and being my lifelong mentor. Soledad Parada and Camila Alfaro for your love and support. Walter Alfaro for leading by example and teaching me the value of hard work. Thank you all so very much. Les amo.

I am also deeply grateful for Teddy Lu, Scott Ternovits and Jon Dien for their input and feedback on the content, Robert Zolna for his help on layout and graphic treatment, Chad Magiera for the photography on page 190.

Thank you.

Andres Parada 2013

andresparada.com
andresparada@live.com

Other BIS Publishers titles of interest:

Sketching, The Basics
ISBN 978 90 6369 253 7
By Koos Eissen and Roselien Steur

Sketching, Drawing techniques for product designers
ISBN 978 90 6369 171 4
By Koos Eissen and Roselien Steur

BIS Publishers
Building Het Sieraad
Postjesweg 1
1057 DT Amsterdam
The Netherlands
T +31 (0)20 515 02 30
F +31 (0)20 515 02 39
bis@bispublishers.nl
www.bispublishers.nl

ISBN 978 90 6369 309 1